LIVING A
PROVIDENTIAL
LIFE

STUDY GUIDE AND JOURNAL

LIVING A PROVIDENTIAL LIFE

STUDY GUIDE AND JOURNAL

BILL WINSCOTT

WESTBOW
PRESS®
A DIVISION OF THOMAS NELSON
& ZONDERVAN

WestBow Press books may be ordered through booksellers or by contacting:

WestBow Press
A Division of Thomas Nelson & Zondervan
1663 Liberty Drive
Bloomington, IN 47403
www.westbowpress.com
844-714-3454

ISBN: 978-1-6642-0538-3 (sc)
ISBN: 978-1-6642-0537-6 (e)

Library of Congress Control Number: 2020917777

Print information available on the last page.

WestBow Press rev. date: 10/21/2020

I dedicate this book to the mentors, leaders, teachers, friends and clergy who have been examples of Christian discipleship over the span of my life. They are responsible for the inspiration and Bible investigation that have given impetus to the writing of this book.

"But the Lord reigns forever, executing judgment from his throne. He will judge the world with justice and rule the nations with fairness. The Lord is a shelter for the oppressed, a refuge in times of trouble. Those who know your name trust in you, for you, O Lord, do not abandon those who search for you." (Ps. 9:7–10)

"And God will generously provide all you need. Then you will always have everything you need and plenty left over to share with others. As the Scriptures say, 'They share freely and give generously to the poor. Their good deeds will be remembered forever.' For God is the one who provides seed for the farmer and then bread to eat. In the same way, he will provide and increase your resources and then produce a great harvest of generosity in you." (2 Cor. 9:8–10)

CONTENTS

SECTION ONE
The Nature of Providence

SECTION TWO
God, Trinity, Scripture and Providence

SECTION THREE
Providence and the Effect on Humans

SECTION FOUR
Providence in Our Lives

Acknowledgements

My wife and family have been of great support and patience in the writing and production process of this book. I am grateful to their encouragement and support in the writing and publishing of this book.

INTRODUCTION

This book is designed for persons interested in living a life more in harmony with God's will. It is structured to assist those that have read the book *Living A Providential Life: Discovering Providential Qualities to Live By* (LAPLB), and desire to mine this subject more deeply and/or utilize the contents in a study setting of one or more people. This study guide will attempt to go deeper and in some cases broader in exploring the subjects contained in *Living A Providential Life: Discovering Providential Qualities to Live By*. The intent here is to provide an organized, in-depth methodology to study the subject by utilizing an interactive approach. Every reader will have different experiences, needs and viewpoint on a subject like this. I know that I have greatly benefited from this approach in my personal study of the Bible and Christian discipleship over the years. I have found that this approach makes this study, "my study." It inevitably becomes a personal journey on the subject through the utilization of an interactive study guide. When used in a group setting this type of study benefits greatly through the multiple experiences and ideas of others. The subject matter here is virtually inexhaustible. Those that have not yet read *Living A Providential Life: Discovering Providential Qualities to Live By* will profit from reading this book, too. May you benefit from this resource in your walk with God.

SECTION ONE

The Nature of Providence

CHAPTER ONE

What Is Providence?

The idea of God's providence manifests itself in a variety of ways. Just a few of these are listed below. Can you explain how these areas bring meaning, importance and substance about the subject to you (LAPLB pp. 1–4)?

Creation

Bible characters

History

Israel

The church

SCRIPTURAL PROVIDENTIAL INSIGHT

> And God will generously provide all you need. Then you will have everything
> you need and plenty left over to share with others. (2 Cor.9:8)

One can view the entire Bible as exhibiting characteristics of God's providence since scripture is seen as one continuous recording of the result of the will of God upon the earth. One way this is manifested is through a historical process that is exemplified in the lives of the many servants of God and the way they bring God's will to the human actions upon the earth.

There are many examples of this throughout the Bible. Can you list six examples of men or women who were servants of God's will in the Old Testament and briefly describe the way they accomplished this?

1.

2.

3.

4.

5.

6.

Scriptural Providential Insight

When the storms of life come, the wicked are whirled away, but the godly have a lasting foundation. (Prov. 10:25)

What was the result of the sins of the wicked during the flood described in Genesis? A person of notable exception to this wickedness was found; "Noah found favor in the sight of the Lord" (Gen. 6:8 HCSB). God assigned an immense task to Noah to save God's created life. "Noah was 600 years old when the flood covered the earth" (Gen. 7:6). Noah partnered with God. "And Noah did this. He did everything that God had commanded him" (Gen. 6:22 HCSB). This is remarkable in so many ways. The complexity and magnitude in constructing an ark 450 feet long and providing for the gathering, space, food, and care for every type of creature is hard to even imagine. What a man Noah must have been! God moved mightily through Noah to accomplish his will upon the earth. Describe below some of the specific acts that Noah accomplished as a partner with God.

We need to recognize that we are limited in our understanding of God's providence. This we need to address early in our study.

What are the best sources (see Ps. 119:32–34) for understanding God's providence (LAPLB pp. 6)?

What is the nature of our limitations in understanding God's providence?

1–My Study Guide Journal

Personal Reflections on My Study of a Providential Life

CHAPTER TWO

Scriptural Observation on the Providence of God

The scriptures provide us with a rich source of material where the providence of God is plainly visible. The lives of the most prominent Bible characters all reflect how God provided them with guidance and assistance as partners for the accomplishment of the will of God. There are so many ways that illustrate the infinite aspects of God's providence found in the Bible. Describe three methods that you find in scripture to illustrate the providence of God at work.

1.

2.

3.

SCRIPTURAL PROVIDENTIAL INSIGHT

Then God said, "I am giving you a sign of my covenant with you and with all living creatures, for all generations to come. I have placed my rainbow in the clouds. It is the sign of my covenant with you and with all the earth. When I send clouds over the earth, the rainbow will appear in the clouds, and I will remember my covenant with you and with all living creatures. Never again will the floodwaters destroy all life. When I see the rainbow in the clouds, I will remember the eternal covenant between God and every living creature on earth. (Gen. 9:12–16)

Reflections on my providential life:

1. What kind of servant or partner am I for God?

2. Do I put God's will first or my own?

3. What has God done for me in the past and present?

4. What priority am I giving to God's will?

5. Am I living within God's design for my life and his will?

Jesus had a high priority for humans to be in harmony with God's will. He explains this in the Lord's Prayer (see Matt. 6:9–13). We are reminded there that we are to pray for God's will to be done on earth. Why? The answer immediately follows that God's will should be done on earth like it is in heaven. This is profound. The length of time we will spend in heaven dwarfs the time we spend on earth. Our time in heaven makes our time spent on earth seem nevertheless brief but consequential. What will heaven be like then? How will the will of God be carried out, and how will this process be different than it is now on earth?

SCRIPTURAL PROVIDENTIAL INSIGHT

I saw no temple in the city, for the Lord God Almighty and the Lamb are its temple. And the city has no need of sun or moon, for the glory of God illuminates the city, and the Lamb is its light. The nations will walk in its light, and the kings of the world will enter the city in all their glory. Its gates will never be closed at the end of day because there will be no night there. And all the nations will bring their glory and honor into the city. Nothing evil will be allowed to enter, nor anyone who practices shameful idolatry and dishonesty but only those whose names are written in the Lamb's Book of Life. (Rev. 21:22–27)

No longer will there be a curse upon anything. For the throne of God and of the Lamb will be there, and his servants will worship him. And they will see his face, and his name will be written on their foreheads. And there will be no night there, no need for lamps or sun for the Lord God will shine on them. And they will reign forever and ever. (Rev. 22:3–5)

Heaven will present an entirely different environment for us. It will be free of sin, death and evil beings. Both the source of and resulting damage from these will disappear. Those written in the Lamb's book of life are the only persons that will be permitted in heaven (see Rev. 21:27). Christ and God the Father will reign forever in heaven. The will of God will be absolute and undisputed. No one who is evil will be allowed in heaven. The children of God who enter heaven will be rewarded according to the deeds they performed on earth (see Rev. 22:12).

PRAYER

Father I pray that my deeds will reflect your will while I reside upon this earth. Grant me the wisdom and discernment to identify your will and act accordingly. Let me have the discipline and obedience to be a true servant and partner in your providence. Give me your grace and strength to perform my task in your honor every day. I pray in the name of Jesus Christ amen.

2–My Study Guide Journal

Personal Reflections on My Study of a Providential Life

CHAPTER THREE

Providence in Nature

Nature illustrates the providence of God in spectacular fashion for all of our senses to absorb and enjoy. We are surrounded every day with the unmistakable presence of a God who has provided us with bountiful evidence of the divine and the careful attention to preserve and sustain this remarkable creation. David's Psalm on the majesty of God's creation details it in a glorious display of presence.

SCRIPTURAL PROVIDENTIAL INSIGHT

O Lord, our Lord, your majestic name fills the earth! Your glory is higher than the heavens. You have taught children and infants to tell of your strength, silencing your enemies and all who oppose you. When I look at the night sky and see the work of your fingers, the moon and the stars you set in place, what are mere mortals that you should think about them, human beings that you should care for them? Yet you made them only a little lower than God and crowned them with glory and honor. You gave them charge of everything you made, putting all things under their authority the flocks and the herds, and all the wild animals, the birds in the sky, the fish in the sea, and everything that swims the ocean currents. O Lord, our Lord, your majestic name fills the earth! (Psalm 8:1–9)

Have you ever glanced skyward on a dark night in a dark location to behold a dome of stars that is just amazing? On such an occasion one can be able to see as many as 2,000 stars. The number of species of plants, animals, birds, and fish is staggering and we are still recording new ones all the time. God's creation of all of these is recorded in the first chapter of Genesis. The creation illustrates the providence of God in a magnificent yet concise and powerful way. Take a minute to reflect upon this through the following questions.

1. What did God provide on day one of creation (see Gen. 1:1–5)?

2. What did God provide on day two of creation (see Gen. 1:6–8)?

3. What did God provide on day three of creation (see Gen. 1:9–13)?

4. What did God provide on day four of creation (see Gen. 1:14–19)?

5. What did God provide on day five of creation (see Gen. 1:20–23)?

6. What did God provide on day six of creation (see Gen. 1:24–31)?

7. What is the significance of day seven of creation (see Gen. 2:1–3)?

The various aspects of nature that were created by God in Genesis come into play over and over throughout scripture. Virtually all of the great characters of the Bible have nature as part of their story with plants, animals, fish or weather involved. Can you think of examples of this with the following characters?

Adam

Noah

Abraham

Isaac

Moses

Jacob

Jonah

Men and women were the greatest of God's creations. Scripture reflects God's great providential care of and the special place that humans hold in the providence of God.

Scriptural Providential Insight

Praise the Lord from the earth, you creatures of the ocean depths, fire and hail, snow and clouds, wind and weather that obey him, mountains and all hills, fruit trees and all cedars, wild animals and all livestock, small scurrying animals and birds, kings of the earth and all people, rulers and judges of the earth, young men and young women, old men and children. Let them all praise the name of the Lord. For his name is very great; his glory towers over the earth and heaven! (Ps. 148:7–13)

And then at last, the sign that the Son of Man is coming will appear in the heavens, and there will be deep mourning among all the peoples of the earth. And they will see the Son of Man on the clouds of heaven with power and great glory. And he will send out his angels with the mighty blast of a trumpet, and they will gather his chosen ones from all over the world from the farthest ends of the earth and heaven. (Matt. 24:30–31)

God's providence exhibited in nature is beyond our scope to fully comprehend and appreciate. It is there challenging the human ability to fully understand. We need to grasp the originator of all created things and the reason they all hold together. This the Bible explains in unambiguous terms. "Christ is the visible image of the invisible God. He existed before anything was created and is supreme over all creation, for through him God created everything in the heavenly realms and on earth. He made the things we can see and the things we can't see such as thrones, kingdoms, rulers, and authorities in the unseen world. Everything was created through him and for him. He existed before anything else, and he holds all things together"

(Col. 1:15–17). Notice that "all things were created through him and for him." This is a very key point that Paul makes here in the letter to the church at Colossae. The fact that creation exists for Jesus Christ brings clarity and focus to the believer and why we should make Christ the Lord of our lives. He deserves all of the praise and glory that we can give him. Why? Because he made all things and manages to keep the infinite universe in a controlled state of being. This is perfectly in coordination with the fact that Jesus came to the earth in human form to save the world and to save you. "He is before all things, and by Him all things hold together" (Col. 1:17 HCSB). The believer's reaction to all of this is reflected in scripture as thanksgiving, worship, obedience, praise and glory.

3–MY STUDY GUIDE JOURNAL

Personal Reflections on My Study of a Providential Life

CHAPTER FOUR

Types of Providence

Theologians have over time examined the subject of providence and identified various types or divisions to assist in our understanding of the subject. There are a broad number of categories and sub-categories that have been addressed. However, we will just study three of the most commonly identified types that are used today. First, God works to preserve the creation that he initiated and cares for it in order to preserve it. Second, God uses creation in a manner that causes the desired results to occur in a process incorporating the freedom God gives to humans. This is referred to as concurrence. God permits us to have a freedom that can fail. Third, God provides guidance and direction for humans in order to achieve desirable results that will glorify God in a process named governance. There are other types of providence that have been included within the description of providence types. However, these three types of providence just mentioned encompass the vast majority of general providential areas. God's providence includes all creation. "The heavens are Yours; the earth also is Yours. The world and everything in it, You founded them" (Ps. 89:11 HCSB). All types of providence are closely related in terms of fulfilling the will of God.

One of the greatest examples of God's providence is found in Psalm 104. List below six specific examples of God's providence found in this Psalm. Include the type of providence that you would classify as: preservation, concurrence or governance.

1.

2.

3.

4.

5.

6.

God works through humans repeatedly in the Bible to achieve his purpose. Great men of the scriptures verify this special purpose and revelation from God.

SCRIPTURAL PROVIDENTIAL INSIGHT

When I think of all this, I, Paul, a prisoner of Christ Jesus for the benefit of you Gentiles assuming, by the way, that you know God gave me the special responsibility of extending his grace to you Gentiles. As I briefly wrote earlier, God himself revealed his mysterious plan to me. As you read what I have written, you will understand my insight into this plan regarding Christ. God did not reveal it to previous generations, but now by his Spirit he has revealed it to his holy apostles and prophets. (Eph. 3:1–5)

God is steadfast in assuring believers of meeting every real need that we have. God provides every need because he already knows our needs before we even are aware of them and certainly before we ask or pray for them. We have a whole range of needs that sometimes fall into different types of providence. Can you think of what some of these different needs that constitute different types of providence are?

SCRIPTURAL PROVIDENTIAL INSIGHT

And why worry about your clothing? Look at the lilies of the field and how they grow. They don't work or make their clothing, yet Solomon in all his glory was not dressed as beautifully as they are. And if God cares so wonderfully for wildflowers that are here today and thrown into the fire tomorrow, he will certainly care for you. Why do you have so little faith? So don't worry about these things, saying, What will we eat? What will we drink? What will we wear? These things dominate the thoughts of unbelievers, but your heavenly Father already knows all your needs. Seek the kingdom of God above all else, and live righteously, and he will give you everything you need. So don't worry about tomorrow, for tomorrow will bring its own worries. Today's trouble is enough for today. (Matt. 6:28–34)

There are so many ways in which God meets our entire spectrum of needs each day. Have you ever stopped to think about all of the needs you had in the last twenty-four hours that were met? Some of these you expected to have met; but, how many times do we have needs that are unexpectedly met? Think also of the many categories of need that you have and the many categories of providence that are necessary to fulfill these needs. Start with the air you breath, the gravity that connects you to the earth, etc. Your real needs are much greater than you even stop to think about. How much do we take for granted here? Worry about all of these things every day would quickly incapacitate any human: "This is why I tell you: Don't worry about your life" (Matt. 6:25 HCSB).

4–My Study Guide Journal

Personal Reflections on My Study of a Providential Life

SECTION TWO

God, Trinity, Scripture and Providence

CHAPTER FIVE

God and Providence

Our God can be described as possessing many significant attributes that theologians go to great lengths in cataloging and expanding upon as an effort to understand the source of divine providence. How can we attempt to understand our God unless we learn his observed characteristics? Scripture gives us many hints of these and revelations that we observe in the world, also. Just a few of these characteristics are:

1. God was not created and relies on nothing else for existence (LAPLB pp. 31). Scripture makes this clear in many places.

SCRIPTURAL PROVIDENTIAL INSIGHT

In the beginning the Word already existed. The Word was with God, and the Word was God. He existed in the beginning with God. God created everything through him, and nothing was created except through him. The Word gave life to everything that was created, and his life brought light to everyone. (John 1:1–4)

What can we assume is true of God from this key scripture?

2. The omnipotence of God is mentioned over and over throughout the Bible. Just a few examples are listed in Job 41; Psalm 145; Isaiah 34; Ezekiel 12; Micah 4; Zechariah 8; Acts 2; Ephesians 6; 1 Thessalonians 4; Hebrews 7 and 2 Peter 3. The majestic power of God is on full display in scripture.

SCRIPTURAL PROVIDENTIAL INSIGHT

It was in the year King Uzziah died that I saw the Lord. He was sitting on a lofty throne, and the train of his robe filled the Temple. Attending him were mighty seraphim, each having six wings. With two wings they covered their faces, with two they covered their feet, and with two they flew. They were calling out to each other. "Holy, holy, holy is the Lord of Heaven's Armies! The whole earth is filled with his glory!" Their voices shook the Temple to its foundation, and the entire building was filled with smoke. Then I said, "It's all over! I am doomed, for I am a sinful man. I have filthy lips, and I live among a people with filthy lips. Yet I have seen the King, the Lord of Heaven's Armies. (Isaiah 6:1–5)

The power of God is fully evident here. No doubt is left concerning the omnipotence of the Almighty Lord of Lords.

What examples do you observe in scripture or in our world that would lead you to conclude that God is omnipotent?

God is a God of the impossible (see Jer. 32:17; Matt. 19:26). Do you have examples of the impossible that God found possible in your life or the lives of others you know?

3. God is eternal and unchanging His message is made known everywhere. "But now as the prophets foretold and as the eternal God has commanded, this message is made known to all Gentiles everywhere, so that they too might believe and obey him" (Rom. 16:26). The word "eternal" or "eternity" is mentioned over one hundred times in scripture. How does this fact support God's eternal characteristic?

4. Our God is omnipresent. He is always with us and ready to help and defend his servants. "God is our refuge and strength, a helper who is always found in times of trouble" (Ps. 46:1 HCSB). Why do you think that certain Bible characters like Adam, Noah, Abraham, Jacob, Isaac, Moses, Paul and John along with God's many prophets were especially aware of this quality of God?

5. Our God is a sovereign God. He is not under anyone or anything. He is in total control of everything in creation. This sovereignty works in coordination with the providence of God and the guidance of his will.

SCRIPTURAL PROVIDENTIAL INSIGHT

For I have come down from heaven to do the will of God who sent me, not to do my own will. And this is the will of God, that I should not lose even one of all those he has given me, but that I should raise them up at the last day. For it is my Father's will that all who see his Son and believe in him should have eternal life. I will raise them up at the last day. (John 6:38–40)

6. There are many more attributes ascribed to God in scripture. Can you use the following list and choose three that mean the most to you in your life and why?

Attributes: Justice, Mercy, Love, Truth, Freedom, Wisdom, Holiness, Spiritual, Peace

1. Attribute

2. Attribute

3. Attribute

The issue of God's divine providence is of critical importance in scripture. One must ask yourself what, why, how and when God acts throughout the Bible to achieve the objectives of his will and providence. Many times this is obvious. However, there are occasions where the will and providence of God just seems to escape the apparent contents of the story. Can you relate below of a Bible story that does not make a lot of sense in relation to God's will and providence; however, upon closer examination clearly comes into focus when viewed from a future perspective?

SCRIPTURAL PROVIDENTIAL INSIGHT

The Lord looks down from heaven and sees the whole human race. From his throne he observes all who live on the earth. He made their hearts, so he understands everything they do. (Ps. 33:13–15)

5–MY STUDY GUIDE JOURNAL

Personal Reflections on My Study of a Providential Life

CHAPTER SIX

The Direction of All Things

We have just observed how God looks down from heaven upon humans and understands everything they do (see Ps. 33:13–15). This is a revelation of God's span of observation and comprehension capabilities. With this capability the directing of all things is made easily attainable. It is hard to fathom how close God is to you and the depth of his love.

SCRIPTURAL PROVIDENTIAL INSIGHT

I can never escape from your Spirit! I can never get away from your presence! If I go up to heaven, you are there; if I go down to the grave you are there. (Ps. 139:7–8)

You watched me as I was being formed in utter seclusion, as I was woven together in the dark of the womb. You saw me before I was born. Every day of my life was recorded in your book. Every moment was laid out before a single day had passed. How precious are your thoughts about me, O God. They cannot be numbered! I can't even count them; they outnumber the grains of sand! And when I wake up, you are still with me! (Ps. 139:15–18)

We cannot escape the presence and attention of God. He has had precious thoughts about you that cannot be numbered. The providential life you will live is already anticipated by a Father who has awareness and thought in every detail of our lives and directs all things. "See if there is any offensive way in me; lead me in the everlasting way" (Ps. 139:24 HCSB). We cannot escape God's presence. "I can never get away from your presence!" (Ps. 139:7). Not only can we not remove ourselves from God; but, the Lord knows us intimately. "O Lord, you have examined my heart and know everything about me" (Ps. 139:1). God has unfailing love for you (see Ps. 138:2). God answers our prayers and encourages us through His strength (see Ps. 138:3). Even though God is great he cares for his humble human creation (Ps. 138:6). The Lord works out his plans for your life (see Ps. 138:8). We see in all of this that God is a personal God and involved in your life in every detail. God cares about you, he loves you and he protects you (1 John 4:10; Ps. 138:7). God ultimately directs all things and works through his creation to achieve his plan. "The Lord will fulfill His purpose for me." (Ps. 138:8 HCSB).

1. How do you feel God has worked his plan through your life?

2. What examples of God's intimacy have you experienced?

3. Can you think of times where you were protected by the Lord in your life?

4. Have you felt God move with faithfulness in your life?

The Apostle Paul illustrates how God works in us to provide direction that we so desperately need in our lives.

SCRIPTURAL PROVIDENTIAL INSIGHT

So then, my dear friends, just as you have always obeyed, not only in my presence, but now even more in my absence, work out your own salvation with fear and trembling. For it is God who is working in you, enabling you both to desire and to work out His good purpose. (Phil. 2:12–13 HCSB)

We must remember that our faithful service is an offering to God (see Phil. 2:17). We need to allow God to transform us into a new person so we will comprehend God's will for us.

SCRIPTURAL PROVIDENTIAL INSIGHT

Don't copy the behavior and customs of this world, but let God transform you into a new person by changing the way you think. Then you will learn to know God's will for you which is good and pleasing and perfect. (Rom. 12:2)

Note that when we know God's will for us we are rewarded in three ways. First, God's will is good for us in every way. Second, God's will is pleasing in our life. Third, God's will is perfect. Now we do not experience many perfect things in our life on earth but we know God's will is perfect! This is worth pausing to consider.

1. Has your life been transformed by God when you came to know Jesus Christ?

2. If so, how was your own life transformed by God after becoming a Christian?

3. Do feel this transformation is an action by God that is still in process?

We can all be involved as servants of Christ in this world. As Paul indicates, we can plant seed and water it but it is God who makes it grow (see 1 Cor. 3:6–9).

Scriptural Providential Insight

So then, since Christ suffered physical pain, you must arm yourselves with the same attitude he had, and be ready to suffer, too. For if you have suffered physically for Christ, you have finished with sin. You won't spend the rest of your lives chasing your own desires, but you will be anxious to do the will of God. (1 Pet. 4:1–2)

1. How do you view the central importance of God's providence (LAPLB pp. 35)?

2. How are the attributes of God discussed in Chapter 5 relate to God's direction of all things?

6–MY STUDY GUIDE JOURNAL

Personal Reflections on my Study of a Providential Life

CHAPTER SEVEN

Providence and the Trinity

We must as Christians be careful to include all three persons of the Trinity in all phases of our Christian witness. The Father, Son and Spirit of the Trinity all participate in vital functions of the overall providence of God. This is seen in the many references expounded upon previously (LAPLB pp. 46–49). It is important that we study the concept of the Trinity in relation to God's providence so that the providential contributions of the Father, Son and Spirit is understood and appreciated.

SCRIPTURAL PROVIDENTIAL INSIGHT

Therefore I also, after I heard of your faith in the Lord Jesus and your love for all the saints, do not cease to give thanks for you, making mention of you in my prayers: that the God of our Lord Jesus Christ, the Father of glory, may give you the spirit of wisdom and revelation in the knowledge of Him, the eyes of your understanding being enlightened; that you may know what is the hope of His calling, what are the riches of the glory of His inheritance in the saints, and what *is* the exceeding greatness of His power toward us who believe, according to the working of His mighty power which He worked in Christ when He raised Him from the dead and seated *Him* at the right hand in the heavenly *places*, far above all principality and power and might and dominion, and every name that is named, not only in this age but also in that which is to come. And He put all *things* under His feet, and gave Him *to be* head over all *things* to the church, which is His body, the fullness of Him who fills all in all. (Eph. 1:15–23 NKJV)

Scripture is clear with the unique responsibilities of providential actions in God's plan.

The Father, Son and Spirit work together in their unique functions to accomplish the providential actions required to accomplish the will of God.

SCRIPTURAL PROVIDENTIAL INSIGHT

But you are not controlled by your sinful nature. You are controlled by the Spirit if you have the Spirit of God living in you. (And remember that those who do not have the Spirit of Christ living in them do not belong to him at all.) And Christ lives within you, so even though your body will die because of sin, the Spirit gives you life because you have been made right with God. The Spirit of God, who raised Jesus from the dead, lives in you. And just as God raised Christ Jesus from the dead, he will give life to your mortal bodies by this same Spirit living within you. (Rom. 8:9–11)

1. Do you feel the Spirit of God living in you?

2. If so, is the Spirit of God controlling you? How?

3. The Spirit living within you will raise you from the dead some day. Do you believe it? (see 1 Thess. 4:13–18). How does this make sense in light of the Spirit's function in the New Testament?

4. What is the single most significant function you see in the providence of the Father, Son and Holy Spirit?

SCRIPTURAL PROVIDENTIAL INSIGHT

But it was to us that God revealed these things by his Spirit. For his Spirit searches out everything and shows us God's deep secrets. No one can know a person's thoughts except that person's own spirit and no one can know God's thoughts except God's own Spirit. And we have received God's Spirit (not the world's spirit), so we can know the wonderful things God has freely given us. (1 Cor. 2:10–12)

We see here the interrelated cooperation and coordination between God the Father and the Holy Spirit, specifically in this case with the providential gifts freely given to us. Numerous references in scripture illustrate the intimate connection between God the Father, God the Son and God the Holy Spirit plus a connection to believers in Jesus Christ. Providence flows to the believer from our trinitarian God (see Rom. 8:9–11).

SCRIPTURAL PROVIDENTIAL INSIGHT

So now you Gentiles are no longer strangers and foreigners. You are citizens along with all of God's holy people. You are members of God's family. Together, we are his house, built on the foundation of the apostles and the prophets. And the cornerstone is Christ Jesus himself. We are carefully joined together in him, becoming a holy temple for the Lord. Through him you Gentiles are also being made part of this dwelling where God lives by his Spirit. (Eph. 2:19–22)

This excerpt from Ephesians is a striking example of how the Trinity works together to achieve the providential plan of God that includes the joining together of humans as "citizens with the saints and members of God's household" and the fact that we are "joined together in Him, becoming a holy temple for the Lord." This small section of scripture involves God the Father, God the Son and God the Holy Spirit in an explanatory description of our relationship with the Trinity. These are truly words to rejoice over!

1. Do you feel like a "citizen along with all of God's holy people?"

2. How do you feel we are "carefully joined together" in Jesus Christ?

3. Christ is compared in Ephesians 2:20 to the cornerstone of God's household. How does this compare with Colossians 2:9? How do these two verses fit together and complement each other?

PRAYER

Father God, we rejoice in selecting believers as "citizens along with all of God's holy people." Although we cannot comprehend the reason this is so or the full significance of this joining together in Jesus Christ, we humbly give our thanks and gratefulness that this is so. We praise you and always praise our Savior, Jesus Christ. We pray in the name of the Father, Son and Holy Spirit amen.

7–MY STUDY GUIDE JOURNAL

Personal Reflections on My Study of a Providential Life

SECTION THREE

Providence and the Effect on Humans

CHAPTER EIGHT

How Does the Providence of God Effect Humans?

Scripture gives us abundant evidence of the providence of God and its effect upon humans.

We can often relate most easily to the providence of God that is evident in the lives of the vivid characters displayed in the Bible. The characters like Noah, Isaac, Jacob, Joseph, Moses, Joshua, Ruth, David, etc. give us a colorful depiction of God's providence that is inescapable. We can laugh, weep, cringe, frown or smile in these stories of how God works through these servants to achieve his will.

Briefly outline God's providence in the lives of the following (LAPLB pp. 53–56):

1. Noah

2. Isaac

3. Joseph

4. Joshua

5. Elijah

6. Ezra

7. Esther

Providence In The Future

God communicates to humans in scripture prophecy and the direct communications contained within scripture. The results of communications concerning the future is referred to as revelation. Approximately one-fourth of the Bible is devoted to this prophetic revelation to humans. Assuming that this large quantity translates to a strong emphasis on the subject, revelation is important! When we examine specific prophecy examples throughout the Word of God we have no doubt that this is the case.

Give three examples of prophecy you feel are particularly important (LAPLB pp. 59–60)?

1.

2.

3.

Providence In Prayer

No other area of our life does God move with more power and presence than in our act of prayer. There are many examples of prayers in the Bible and how God moves in reaction to these prayers. One of my favorite examples is in Genesis 24 where Abraham's servant prays for God's assistance in finding a wife for his master, Isaac. Note here that Abraham had already informed the servant of the help the Lord will provide. "He will send his angel ahead of you, and he will see to it that you find a wife there for my son" (Gen. 24:7).

Scriptural Providential Insight

O Lord, God of my master, Abraham," he prayed. "Please give me success today, and show unfailing love to my master, Abraham. See, I am standing here beside this spring, and the young women of the town are coming out to draw water. This is my request. I will ask one of them, 'Please give me a drink from your jug.' If she says, 'Yes, have a drink, and I will water your camels, too!' – let her be the one you have selected as Isaac's wife. This is how I will know that you have shown unfailing love to my master." Before he had finished praying, he saw a young woman named Rebekah coming out with her water jug on her shoulder. (Gen. 24:12–15)

Describe below some examples of the subject of prayers you have prayed and had answered prayer in your life or those you know (LAPLB pp. 60–63)?

PROVIDENCE IN MIRACLES

The Bible documents many miracles that are stunning in their nature: the sun and moon holding still in the sky (see Josh. 10:13), the miraculous signs God used against the Egyptians (see Num. 14:22), the many miracles of Jesus (see John 11:47), and the miracles of Paul (see Acts 15:12). The reason for these are implied and specifically recorded in some cases. "At the same time, God also testified by signs and wonders, various miracles, and distributions of gifts from the Holy Spirit according to His will" (Heb. 2:4 HCSB).

1. Do you think miracles still occur in our world today? Why? (LAPLB pp. 63–64)?

2. What is your favorite example of a miraculous event recorded in scripture?

3. How do miracles fit into God's providential plan?

SCRIPTURAL PROVIDENTIAL INSIGHT

I tell you the truth, anyone who believes in me will do the same works I have done, and even greater works, because I am going to be with the Father. You can ask for anything in my name, and I will do it, so that the Son can bring glory to the Father. Yes, ask me for anything in my name, and I will do it! (John 14:12–14)

As Paul spoke on and on, a young man named Eutychus, sitting on the windowsill, became very drowsy. Finally, he fell sound asleep and dropped three stories to his death below. Paul went down, bent over him, and took him into his arms. "Don't worry," he said, "he's alive!" Then they all went back upstairs, shared in the Lord's Supper, and ate together. Paul continued talking to them until dawn and then he left. Meanwhile the young man was taken home alive and well, and everyone was greatly relieved. (Acts 20:9–12)

8–My Study Guide Journal

Personal Reflections on My Study of a Providential Life

CHAPTER NINE

Angels and God's Divine Providence

The use of angels to effect the purpose of God's providence is well-documented throughout scripture. These created beings are ideal for the many functions required by God to accomplish a wide range of tasks (LAPLB pp. 65–66).

Describe the function of angels in the following Bible references?

1. Judges 6

2. 2 Chronicles 21

3. Acts 27:23–24

SCRIPTURAL PROVIDENTIAL INSIGHT

While Zechariah was in the sanctuary, an angel of the Lord appeared to him, standing to the right of the incense altar. Zechariah was shaken and overwhelmed with fear when he saw him. But the angel said, Don't be afraid Zechariah! God has heard your prayer. Your wife Elizabeth, will give you a son, and you are to name him John. You will have great joy and gladness, and many will rejoice at his birth, for he will be great in the eyes of the Lord. He must never touch wine or other alcoholic drinks. He will be filled with the Holy Spirit, even before his birth. And he will turn many Israelites to the Lord their God. He will be a man with the spirit and power of Elijah. He will prepare the people for the coming of the Lord. He will turn the hearts of the fathers to their children, and he will cause those who are rebellious to accept the wisdom of the godly. (Luke 1:11–17)

This reference from Luke describes one of the most important functions that any angel was tasked to perform. The angel Gabriel insured that Zechariah believed his words as we discover in the following verses (see Luke 1:19–20). Many notable observations can be observed in these few verses. First, Zechariah was filled with fear at the presence of the angel. This was an uncommon reaction as we see in other scriptures involving angels. Second, we see assurance from the angel and a reference that God is responsible for the angelic appearance because of answered prayer. Three, the angel gives specific instructions to Zechariah. Four, the angel provides the servant Zechariah with prophetic information. Five, Gabriel informs Zechariah that he stands in the very presence of God. Six, it is also important to notice here what type of people Zechariah and his wife, Elizabeth were. "Both were righteous in God's sight, living without blame according to all the commands and requirements of the Lord" (Luke 1:6 HCSB).

9–MY STUDY GUIDE JOURNAL

Personal Reflections on My Study of a Providential Life

Chapter Ten

Evil, Sin and Providence

The problem of sin and evil is an integral part of the story of the Bible from beginning to the end. God provides for the solution to evil and sin through repentance and a saving knowledge of Jesus Christ. God is a perfect, holy and loving God who cannot tolerate sin and evil and loves His human creation so much that the Son of God died for our sins. This is the overarching story of all scripture. In order to understand evil and sin it is helpful to understand four perspectives of it in Scripture. First, we need to review how sin came into the world originally (see Gen. 3:1–8). Second, we must understand the long-term relationship between Satan and humans that God ordains (see Gen. 3:15). Third, we should look at the relationship between God and Satan and how Satan thinks and acts (see Job 1:6–12). Fourth, we need to remind ourselves of the ultimate fate of Satan, evil, death and suffering (see Rev. 20:7–10; 21:4).

Scriptural Providential Insight

> And all the nations will bring glory and honor into the city. Nothing evil will be allowed to enter, nor anyone who practices shameful idolatry and dishonesty, but only those whose names are written in the Lamb's book of life. (Rev. 21:26–27)

Here we see that evil will not be allowed to enter the city of the New Jerusalem in heaven.

Evil will have been eliminated totally. No one in heaven will be exposed any longer to evil, sin and death.

How is evil perpetuated in these references? What are the consequences?

1. Numbers 14:26–30

2. 2 Samuel 24:10–25

3. Daniel 6:19–27

Scripture is clear that evil and sin is a constant threat in our lives and we must battle it at all times. "'The Lord asked Satan, 'Where have you come from?' 'From roaming through the earth,' Satan answered Him, and walking around on it'" (Job 2:2 HCSB).

SCRIPTURAL PROVIDENTIAL INSIGHT

So we must listen very carefully to the truth we have heard, or we may drift away from it. For the message God delivered through angels has always stood firm, and every violation of the law and every act of disobedience was punished. So what makes us think we can escape if we ignore this great salvation that was first announced by the Lord Jesus himself and then delivered to us by those who heard him speak? And God confirmed the message by giving signs and wonders and various miracles and gifts of the Holy Spirit whenever he chose. (Heb. 2:1–4)

Notice in this reference from the book of Hebrews all persons of the Trinity work together to keep the human creation on course with God's salvation and will for us. We are cautioned to listen to the truth which guards us from deviating from our way in Christ. God confirmed the message of Jesus Christ with signs, wonders, miracles and gifts of the Holy Spirit. God makes it virtually impossible for us to stray from the truth without knowing what the truth consists of unless we reject all sources of truth outright.

What has been your most difficult problem with sin and evil in your life?

What are the most vivid examples you can recall in your life or the life of others with sin and evil?

How do you see sin and evil impacting the world on a global scale today?

10–MY STUDY GUIDE JOURNAL

Personal Reflections on My Study of a Providential Life

SECTION FOUR

Providence in Our Lives

CHAPTER ELEVEN

The Qualities of Providential Living

Scripture presents the reader with a number of clear qualities that personify a person that believes and honors Jesus Christ and God the Father. These qualities are illuminated in the lives of biblical characters and in the life of Christ. The qualities of a believer bear examination and study for these characteristics all emanate from God and Christ. Christ exemplified these qualities while on earth for our future adoption and imitation. Look at how an individual like Saul, a self-righteous Jewish religious leader, became Paul, the humble Christian who worked tirelessly for the spread of the church as an example of the qualities that Christ displayed. Paul had many self-proclaimed problems of his own as a mere mortal, but his desire and effort to exemplify the Christian qualities was relentless. In the following pages we will explore these Christian qualities. I would encourage you to make this study and journal deeply personal and candid in your approach. By doing this you will maximize the usefulness of this exercise. Prayerfully consider the application of each quality in your daily living. The applications of all of these qualities are impossible without the help of the Holy Spirit working in your life. The study in scripture of each quality will bring them into focus as a potentially achievable goal for your life with the help of God. Just the associated scripture attached to these qualities will help in your understanding of the Bible.

1. A believer is relatively powerless without **discipline** in their life as described in scripture. We are to have discipline as a Christian in order to avoid sin and live in holiness.

SCRIPTURAL PROVIDENTIAL INSIGHT

God's will is for you to be holy, so stay away from all sexual sin. Then each of you will control his own body and live in holiness and honor not in lustful passion like the pagans who do not know God and his ways. (1 Thess. 4:3 – 5)

God has called us to live holy lives, not impure lives. Therefore, anyone who refuses to live by these rules is not disobeying human teaching but is rejecting God, who gives his Holy Spirit to you. (1 Thess. 4:7–8)

Joyful are those you discipline, Lord, those you teach with your instructions. You give them relief from troubled times until a pit is dug to capture the wicked. (Ps. 94:12–13)

Questions:

1.) Where are you at with the quality of discipline? What specific areas could you improve upon here?

2.) What does scripture say about how to improve your discipline (see Prov. 19:18,20; Col. 2:5; Heb. 12:7)?

3.) Why is discipline necessary to living the providential life?

2. **Faith** represents a bedrock necessity to the Christian believer. We must begin with the idea of faith as we progress in the Christian life. Otherwise, what can we base our process of devotion to Christ upon? Faith is mentioned in the Bible over 250 times. Faith is essential for any Christian.

Scriptural Providential Insight

Through Him we have received grace and apostleship for obedience to the faith among all nations for His name, among whom you also are the called of Jesus Christ. (Rom. 1:5 NKJV)

This Good News tells us how God makes us right in his sight. This is accomplished from start to finish by faith. As the Scriptures say, "It is through faith that a righteous person has life." (Rom. 1:17)

For yet in a very little while, the Coming One will come and not delay. But My righteous one will live by faith; and if he draws back, I have no pleasure in him. (Heb. 10:37–38 HCSB)

Questions:

1.) Where are you at with the quality of faith? What specific areas could you improve upon here?

2.) What does scripture say about how to improve faith in your life (see Exod. 14:31; Matt. 17:20; Acts 14:27; Rom. 4:9; 14:23; 1 Cor. 16:13; 2 Tim. 1:5; Gal. 3:24)?

3.) Why is this quality of faith necessary to living the providential life?

3. **Redemption** is the gift of God made possible through the blood of Christ on the cross. This is the supreme gift to humans. A gift so incredible that our minds cannot fathom the nature of the redemptive implications from God.

SCRIPTURAL PROVIDENTIAL INSIGHT

No eye has seen, no ear has heard, and no mind has imagined what God has prepared for those who love him. But it was to us that God revealed these things by his Spirit. For his Spirit searches out everything and shows us God's deep secrets. No one can know a person's thoughts except that person's own spirit, and no one can know God's thoughts except God's own Spirit. And we have received God's Spirit (not the world's spirit), so we can know the wonderful things God has freely given us. (1 Cor. 2:9–12)

He is the down payment of our inheritance, for the redemption of the possession, to the praise of His glory. (Eph. 1:14 HCSB)

Questions:

1.) Where are you at with the quality of redemption? What specific areas could you improve upon here and enrich your life?

2.) What does scripture say about redemption in your life (see Ps. 111:9; Luke 21:28; Rom. 3:24; Eph. 4:30; Col. 1:14; Heb. 9:12)?

3.) Why is this quality necessary to living the providential life? What would Christianity mean without redemption?

4. **Eternal life** is available through Jesus Christ for all who believe. We are taught by Christ to "rejoice because your names are registered in heaven" (Luke 10:20). Believers are already enjoying eternal life. Yes, they will experience physical death. But, they will go on to experience eternity in heaven through the sacrificial act of Jesus on the cross.

Scriptural Providential Insight

Physical training is good, but training for godliness is much better, promising benefits in this life and in the life to come. This is a trustworthy saying, and everyone should accept it. This is why we work hard and continue to struggle, for our hope is in the living God, who is the Savior of all people and particularly of all believers. (1 Tim. 4:8–10)

He generously poured out the Spirit upon us through Jesus Christ our Savior. Because of his grace he made us right in his sight and gave us confidence that we will inherit eternal life. (Titus 3:6–8)

Questions:

1.) Where are you at with the quality of eternal life? What does this feature of a Christian life mean to you? How does this impact your daily life?

2.) What does scripture say about eternal life (see Matt. 19:16–26; John 5:24; Heb. 5:9; 1 John 5:11, 20)?

3.) Why is this quality necessary to living the providential life? What would Christianity mean without the reward of eternal life?

5. The **kingdom of God** is a kingdom based upon God's rule that extends through all generations that includes all who do right and excludes all those who do wrong (see 1 Cor. 6:9–11). The kingdom of God is central to the will of God. The promised time of the kingdom of God was announced by Jesus (see Mark 1:15).

Scriptural Providential Insight

I want you all to know about the miraculous signs and wonders the Most High God has performed for me. How great are his signs, how powerful his wonders! His kingdom will last forever, his rule through all generations. (Dan. 4:2–3)

You will conceive and give birth to a son, and you will name him Jesus. He will be very great and will be called the Son of the Most High. The Lord God will give him the throne of his ancestor David. And he will reign over Israel forever; his kingdom will never end! (Luke 1:31–33)

Questions:

1.) How are you being impacted in your life by the kingdom of God? What specific areas would you change to improve the kingdom enrichment in your life?

2.) What does scripture say about the kingdom of God in your life (see Luke 9:60; Rom. 14:17–18; 2 Thess. 1:5; John 3:3–5; Ps. 145:13; Luke 11:20)?

3.) Why is this quality necessary to living the providential life? What would Christianity mean without the kingdom of God?

6. God provides **daily needs** for all of His children. The Bible tells the story of God providing for His human creations from Genesis to Exodus. God tenderly provided clothes for Adam and Eve after their fall in Genesis 3:21. God provides light so there is no night in heaven in Revelation 22:5.

SCRIPTURAL PROVIDENTIAL INSIGHT

That is why I tell you not to worry about everyday life, whether you have enough food and drink or enough clothes to wear. Isn't life more than food, and your body more than clothing? (Matt. 6:25)

The Lord is my shepherd; there is nothing I lack. (Ps. 23:1 HCSB)

Share with the saints in their needs; pursue hospitality. (Rom. 12:13 HCSB)

Questions:

1.) What are your daily needs? Is God meeting your daily needs? Do you ask God to meet other needs too?

2.) What does scripture say about meeting daily needs in your life? (see Phil. 4:19; 2 Cor. 9:8; Hebrews 13:21)?

3.) Why is this quality of meeting daily needs necessary to living the providential life? What would Christianity mean without God meeting basic needs?

7. **Prayer** is a privileged form of direct communications to God. We are urged in scripture to pray often and for everything. Our life is in need of prayer and communion with the Lord that is a source of grace and goodness for those that practice it. Prayer adds a dimension of faith we cannot obtain in any other way.

Scriptural Providential Insight

Rejoice in hope; be patient in affliction; be persistent in prayer. (Rom. 12:12 HCSB)

Pray at all times in the Spirit with every prayer and request, and stay alert in this with all perseverance and intercession for all the saints. (Eph. 6:18 HCSB)

I tell you, you can pray for anything, and if you believe that you've received it, it will be yours. But when you are praying, first forgive anyone you are holding a grudge against, so that your Father in heaven will forgive your sins, too. (Mark 11:24)

Questions:

1.) How is your prayer life? Do you feel comfortable in the act of prayer? Do you track the results of your prayers?

2.) What does scripture say about prayer in our lives (see Matt. 11:25; Acts 1:14; Rom. 8:26–27; 12:12; Phil. 4:6; Col. 4:2; 1 Thess. 5:16; James 5:13; Jude 1:20)?

3.) Why is this quality of prayer necessary to living the providential life? What would Christianity mean without the quality of prayer in a believer's life?

8. **God's presence** is assured to the believer in scripture. Our God desires to be in fellowship with you in an incomprehensible love that will never fail to support and sustain us. Even when we run from God as Jonah did, God finds us and rescues us in order for His will to be accomplished. (see Jon. 1:3–4).

Scriptural Providential Insight

Make a joyful noise to the Lord, all the earth! Serve the Lord with gladness! Come into his presence with singing! (Ps. 100:1–2 ESV)

Since we have the same spirit of faith according to what has been written, "I believed, and so I spoke, we also believe, and so we also speak, knowing that he who raised the Lord Jesus will raise us also with Jesus and bring us with you into his presence." (2 Cor. 4:13–14 ESV)

For Christ has entered, not into holy places made with hands, which are copies of the true things, but into heaven itself, now to appear in the presence of God on our behalf. (Heb. 9:24 ESV)

Questions:

1.) Do you feel you experience the presence of God in your life every day?

2.) What does scripture say about being in the presence of God (see Ps. 139:7; John 16:17–19; 2 Thess. 1:9)?

3.) Why is this quality of God's presence to living the providential life? What would Christianity mean without God's presence in our lives?

9. **Focus** on Jesus and his mission in the world every day. Jesus asks that we devote our whole lives in faith to acknowledge Him as our Savior. The saving of believers in Christ has come at great cost and sacrifice as part of God's plan and will. This demands focus in our lives to acknowledge Christ and His will in our lives.

Scriptural Providential Insight

Stay awake and pray so that you won't enter into temptation. The spirit is willing, but the flesh is weak. (Mark 14:38 HCSB)

Hold on to the pattern of wholesome teaching you learned from me, a pattern shaped by the faith and love that you have in Christ Jesus. Through the power of the Holy Spirit who lives within us, carefully guard the precious truth that has been entrusted to you. (2 Tim. 1:13–14)

For we have become companions of the Messiah if we hold firmly until the end the reality that we had at the start. (Heb. 3:14 HCSB)

Questions:

1.) Do you feel you focus on Christ every day? What temptations can interfere?

2.) What does scripture say about having a focus on Christ (see Matt. 28:18–20; Matt. 10:38–39; John 14:13–14; 15:10; 17:20–21; 1 Pet. 3:15; Rev. 22:4)?

3.) Why is this quality of focus important to living the providential life? What would Christianity mean without focus on Christ in our lives? What helps you focus on Christ?

10. **Wisdom** is a Christian quality that is mentioned throughout scripture with great frequency. This quality is connected closely with knowledge, instruction and judgment. Scripture speaks to all of these attributes because that is the purpose of the Bible. The book of Proverbs is especially rich in mentioning this quality.

SCRIPTURAL PROVIDENTIAL INSIGHT

The lips of the wise broadcast knowledge, but not so the heart of fools. (Prov. 15:7 HCSB)

Who is like the wise person, and who knows the interpretation of a matter? A man's wisdom brightens his face, and the sternness of his face is changed. (Eccles. 8:1 HCSB)

Therefore, everyone who hears these words of Mine and acts on them will be like a sensible man who built his house on the rock. (Matt. 7:24 HCSB)

Questions:

1.) Do you many times feel the wisdom that the scriptures impart to you? What practical effect does this wisdom have upon your life?

2.) What does scripture say about being wise (see Eccles. 10:2; Matt. 11:19; Luke 1:17; Acts 6:10; 1 Cor. 2:6–7, 13; Col. 1:28)?

3.) Why is this quality of wisdom vital to living the providential life? What would Christianity mean without spiritual wisdom? What helps you in obtaining wisdom?

11.1–MY STUDY GUIDE JOURNAL

Personal Reflections on My Study of a Providential Life

Discipline

Redemption

Kingdom of God

Prayer

Focus

Faith

Eternal Life

Daily Needs

Presence

Wisdom

11. **Comfort** is provided by God through a believer's faith. This comfort nurtured the beginning days of the church and caused it to multiply in size (see Acts 9:31). Our comfort rests on our faith and the peace with God that comforts us and comes through the Lord Jesus Christ (see Rom. 5:1).

SCRIPTURAL PROVIDENTIAL INSIGHT

I cried out, "I am slipping!" but your unfailing love, O Lord supported me. When doubts filled my mind, your comfort gave me renewed hope and cheer. (Ps. 94:18–19)

Those who mourn are blessed, for they will be comforted. (Matt. 5:4 HCSB)

All praise to God, the Father of our Lord Jesus Christ. God is our merciful Father and the source of all comfort. He comforts us in all our troubles so that we can comfort others. When they are troubled we will be able to give them the same comfort God has given us. (2 Cor. 1:3–4)

Questions:

1.) Do you many times feel in need of comforting? What is it about Christ that provides comfort to you in times of need?

2.) What does scripture say about the comfort of God (see Ps. 71:19–21; 2 Cor. 1:7; Col. 4:11)?

3.) Why is this quality of comfort that is important to living the providential life? What would Christianity mean without the comfort of God through Christ?

12. **Grace** is the unmerited love, compassion and goodness of God bestowed to humans through Jesus Christ. It is a word used frequently throughout the New Testament and found rarely in the Gospels or in the Old Testament. However, the concept is frequently found throughout scripture. This grace toward men, so visible in the New Testament, originates in God's providence through Jesus Christ.

SCRIPTURAL PROVIDENTIAL INSIGHT

And the Word became flesh and dwelt among us, and we have seen his glory, glory as of the only Son from the Father, full of grace and truth. (John 1:14 ESV)

And from his fullness we have all received, grace upon grace. For the law was given through Moses; grace and truth came through Jesus Christ. (John 1:16–17 ESV)

Questions:

1.) Do you feel the grace of Jesus Christ? What is it about this grace that seems to really impact your life the most?

2.) What does scripture say about grace (see Rom. 12:6; 2 Cor. 9:14; Eph. 2:8; 2 Tim. 1:9; Heb. 4:16; James 4:6; 1 Pet. 4:10; 2 Pet. 3:18)?

3.) Why is this quality of grace important to living the providential life? What would Christianity mean without the grace of God through Christ?

13. **Justification** is made possible through the gift that Christ provided us on the cross. Our faith in Christ allows our sins to be cleansed and our position changed through grace to a justified believer before God. This is a free gift through Christ that simply demands our repentance, hope, love and faith in Jesus.

SCRIPTURAL PROVIDENTIAL INSIGHT

Yet we know that a person is not justified by works of the law but through faith in Jesus Christ, so we also have believed in Christ Jesus, in order to be justified by faith in Christ and not by works of the law, because by works of the law no one will be justified. (Gal. 2:16 ESV)

Now before faith came, we were held captive under the law, imprisoned until the coming faith would be revealed. So then, the law was our guardian until Christ came, in order that we might be justified by faith. (Gal. 3:23–24 ESV)

I tell you, on the day of judgment people will give account for every careless word they speak, for by your words you will be justified, and by your words you will be condemned. (Matt. 12:36–37 ESV)

Questions:

1.) Do you feel your justification through Jesus Christ? What is it about this justification that really impacts your life the most?

2.) What does scripture say about justification (see Rom. 4:25; 2 Cor. 3:9; Gal. 2:21)?

3.) Why is this quality of justification important to living the providential life? What would Christianity mean without the justification by God through Christ?

14. **Sanctification** is when through the sacrifice of Jesus Christ a Christian is set apart in holiness and apart from sin, evil and immorality. We are called to be set free from the sin and evil of this world. This sanctification is a once and for all act through the sacrifice of Jesus Christ.

SCRIPTURAL PROVIDENTIAL INSIGHT

And by that will we have been sanctified through the offering of the body of Jesus Christ once for all (Heb. 10:10 ESV).

I am speaking in human terms, because of your natural limitations. For just as you once presented your members as slaves to impurity and to lawlessness leading to more lawlessness, so now present your members as slaves to righteousness leading to sanctification (Rom. 6:19 ESV).

Sanctify them in the truth; your word is truth. As you sent me into the world, so I have sent them into the world. And for their sake I consecrate myself, that they also may be sanctified in truth (John 17:17–19 ESV).

Questions:

1.) Do you feel your sanctification through Jesus Christ? What is it about sanctification that seems to really impact your life the most?

2.) What does scripture say about sanctification (see Rom. 6:22; 1 Cor. 1:30; 2 Thess. 2:13)?

3.) Why is this quality of sanctification important to living the providential life? What would Christianity mean without the sanctification of God through Christ?

15. **Righteousness** is described in Romans 4 as applied to Abraham and his faith. We see there that Abraham's faith never waivered in believing the promise God made to him. In this way he "brought glory to God." "And because of Abraham's faith, God counted him as righteous" (Rom. 4:22).

SCRIPTURAL PROVIDENTIAL INSIGHT

And when God counted him as righteous, it wasn't just for Abraham's benefit. It was recorded for our benefit, too, assuring us that God will also count us as righteous if we believe in him, the one who raised Jesus our Lord from the dead. He was handed over to die because of our sins, and he was raised to life to make us right with God. (Rom. 4:23–25)

Since you have heard about Jesus and have learned the truth that comes from him, throw off your old sinful nature and your former way of life, which is corrupted by lust and deception. Instead, let the Spirit renew your thoughts and attitudes. Put on your new nature, created to be like God, truly righteous and holy. (Eph. 4:21–24)

Questions:

1.) Do you feel the righteousness through Jesus Christ? What is it about righteousness that seems to really impact your life the most?

2.) What does scripture say about righteousness (see Ps. 111:3; Jer. 23:6; John 16:8; Phil. 3:6; 2 Tim. 4:8; Heb 11:7)?

3.) Why is this quality of righteousness important to living the providential life? What would Christianity mean without the righteousness of God through Christ?

16. **Spiritual satisfaction** is a result of knowing Jesus Christ as your Savior. It is interesting to note the part that satisfaction functions in the beatitudes. God blesses those that come to Christ and the believer experiences satisfaction. The beginning of the Sermon on the Mount addresses the followers of Jesus Christ and the areas of needs requiring satisfaction. However, the key area of need is spiritual in nature.

SCRIPTURAL PROVIDENTIAL INSIGHT

Blessed are those who hunger and thirst for righteousness, for they shall be satisfied. (Matt. 5:6 ESV)

God blesses you who are hungry now, for you will be satisfied. (Luke 6:21)

Jesus replied, "I am the bread of life. Whoever comes to me will never be hungry again. Whoever believes in me will never be thirsty." (John 6:35)

Questions:

1.) Do you feel spiritual satisfaction through Jesus Christ? What is it about spiritual satisfaction that seems to really impact your life the most?

2.) What does scripture say about spiritual satisfaction (see Ps. 63:5; John 6:32–35, 58; Phil. 4:19)?

3.) Why is this quality of spiritual satisfaction that is important to living the providential life? What would Christianity mean without the spiritual satisfaction of God through Christ?

17. **Life in the Spirit** is necessary for living the providential life. All believers have the Spirit of God living in them and supporting them. The Spirit of God gives us life just as when Jesus Christ was raised from the dead. It is the power of the Spirit that puts deeds of sin to death. We receive the Holy Spirit as we are adopted as God's own children.

SCRIPTURAL PROVIDENTIAL INSIGHT

And Christ lives within you, so even though your body will die because of sin, the Spirit gives you life because you have been made right with God. The Spirit of God, who raised Jesus from the dead, lives in you. And just as God raised Christ Jesus from the dead, he will give life to your mortal bodies by the same Spirit living within you. (Rom. 8:10–11)

As for us, we can't help but thank God for you, dear brothers and sisters loved by the Lord. We are always thankful that God chose you to be among the first to experience salvation, a salvation that came through the Spirit who makes you holy and through your belief in the truth. (2 Thess. 2:13)

Questions:

1.) Do you feel life in the Spirit? What is it about life in the Spirit that seems to really impact your life the most?

2.) What does scripture say about life in the Spirit (see Rom. 8:3–4; 1 Cor. 2: 4–5; 1 Cor. 2:12; 2 Cor. 1:21–22; 5 Gal. 3:1–5; 1 Thess. 1:4–5)?

3.) Why is this quality of life in the Spirit that is important to living the providential life? What would Christianity mean without life in the Spirit of God?

18. There is **no separation from God**. As a believer in Jesus Christ we cannot be separated from the love of God. Believers are predestined, called, justified and eventually glorified according to the magnificent sovereignty that God works through all things. Believers belong to Christ, Christ belongs to God and the Spirit of God dwells in us.

Scriptural Providential Insight

Everything belongs to you, and you belong to Christ, and Christ belongs to God. (1 Cor. 3:22–23)

I am praying not only for these disciples but also for all who will ever believe in me through their message. I pray that they will all be one, just as you and I are one, as you are in me, Father, and I am in you. And may they be in us so that the world will believe you sent me. (John 17:20–21)

Don't you realize that all of you together are the temple of God and that the Spirit of God lives in you? (1 Cor. 3:16)

Questions:

1.) Do you feel that you are one with God through the Holy Spirit in you? What is it about life with no separation from God that seems to really impact your life the most?

2.) What does scripture say about a believers not being separated from God (see Rom. 8:38–39; 1 Cor. 3:21–23; John 17:23–26; Eph. 4:20–24; Rev. 22:14)?

3.) Why is this quality of the lack of separation from God that is important to living the providential life? What would Christianity mean without being with God, always?

19. Christ **ended our slavery to the law** and brought righteousness to the believer. Through the sacrifice of Jesus Christ we no longer are under the slavery of the law. We are now dependent only upon the mercy and grace offered in the freedom of the kingdom of God. The law was only a preliminary preparation for the perfection represented by Jesus Christ.

Scriptural Providential Insight

Now you are no longer a slave but God's own child. And since you are his child. God has made you his heir. (Gal. 4:7)

So Christ has truly set us free. Now make sure that you stay free, and don't get tied up again in slavery to the law. (Gal. 5:1)

But there is another power within me that is at war with my mind. This power makes me a slave to the sin that is still within me. Oh, what a miserable person I am! Who will free me from this life that is dominated by sin and death? Thank God! The answer is in Jesus Christ our Lord. (Rom. 7:23–25)

Questions:

1.) Do you feel your life has ended slavery to the law because of Jesus Christ? What is it about life free of slavery to the law that seems to really impact your life the most?

2.) What does scripture say about life that is free from slavery to the law (see Rom. 8:15; 10:4; Gal. 4:4–7; Heb. 10:1; Jer. 31:34)?

3.) Why is this quality of life free from slavery to the law that is important to living the providential life? What would Christianity mean without freedom from the law?

20. People of God have a **special relationship** that is made possible only through Jesus Christ. Honor from God is reserved for those who serve Jesus Christ. Beautiful examples of this special relationship that God has with those who believe are documented throughout scripture. Every prominent figure in the Bible involved in carrying out the will of God is witness to a special relationship.

Scriptural Providential Insight

Anyone who wants to serve me must follow me, because my servants must be where I am. And the Father will honor anyone who serves me. (John 12:26)

Peter replied, "Each of you must repent of your sins and turn to God, and be baptized in the name of Jesus Christ for the forgiveness of your sins. Then you will receive the gift of the Holy Spirit. This promise is to you, to your children, and to those far away, all who have been called by the Lord our God." (Acts 2:38–39)

Questions:

1.) Do you feel you have a special relationship with God because of Jesus Christ? What is it about your special relationship with God that seems to really impact your life the most?

2.) What does scripture say about a person's special relationship with God through Jesus Christ (see John 13:13, 15:26, 16:14; Rom. 9:26; Eph. 3:6; 1 John 4:7)?

3.) What is this quality of having a special relationship with God that is important to living the providential life? What would Christianity mean without our special relationship with Christ?

11.2–My Study Guide Journal

Personal Reflections on My Study of a Providential Life

Comfort	**Spiritual Satisfaction**
Grace	**Life in the Spirit**
Justification	**No Separation from God**
Sanctification	**No Slavery to the Law**
Righteousness	**Special Relationship to God**

21. **Peace** was brought to the earth through Jesus Christ. The quality of peace is mentioned throughout the scriptures as one that applies to those acting in the will of God. The word peace is mentioned over three hundred times in the Bible. We are told that God blesses those that work for peace.

Scriptural Providential Insight

God blesses those who work for peace, for they will be called the children of God. (Matt. 5:9)

Look at those who are honest and good, for a wonderful future awaits those who love peace. (Ps. 37:37)

For Christ himself has brought peace to us. He united Jews and Gentiles into one people when, in his own body on the cross, he broke down the wall of hostility that separated us. (Eph. 2:14)

Questions:

1.) Do you feel a peace because of the work Jesus Christ accomplished on earth? What is it about your peace with God that seems to really impact your life the most?

2.) What does scripture say about a person's peace with God through Jesus Christ (see Mark. 9:50; Luke 1:79; John 16:33; Rom. 5:1; 1 Cor. 14:33; Eph. 6:15; Phil. 4:7; 1 Pet. 3:11)?

3.) Why is this quality of having peace important to living the providential life? What would Christianity mean without peace in our lives?

22. **Truth** is explained in the seventeenth chapter of the book of John as God's word. Truth is pursued throughout the world. Even Pilate was interested in what the nature of truth was, although he was not perceptive enough to recognize it as Jesus plainly explained it. Many people say they are interested in what is truth. The question is would they recognize it if they found it?

Scriptural Providential Insight

Pilate said, "So you are a king?" Jesus responded, "You say I am a king. Actually, I was born and came into the world to testify to the truth. All who love the truth recognize that what I say is true." (John 18:37)

We faithfully preach the truth. God's power is working in us. We use the weapons of righteousness in the right hand for attack and the left hand for defense. (2 Cor. 6:7)

Make them holy by your truth; teach them your word, which is truth. (John 17:17)

Questions:

1.) Do you feel Jesus Christ accomplished truth on earth? What is it about the truth which is represented in God's word that seems to really impact your life the most?

2.) What does scripture say about the truth of God (see Isa. 45:19; John 4:23; 8:32; 15:26; Rom. 1:18; 1 Cor. 13:4–6; Heb. 10:26)?

3.) Why is this quality of having truth important to living the providential life? What would Christianity mean without truth?

23. **Purity** is a basic and important quality for Christians. Scripture is concerned with this from Genesis to Revelation. The process of becoming a believer is one that lends itself to one of purification. As sinners we all need to be conscious of the need to purify ourselves.

SCRIPTURAL PROVIDENTIAL INSIGHT

Once a year Aaron must purify the altar by smearing its horns with blood from the offering made to purify the people from their sin. This will be a regular, annual event from generation to generation, for this is the Lord's most holy altar. (Exod. 30:10)

We prove ourselves by our purity, our understanding, our patience, our kindness, by the Holy Spirit within us, and by our sincere love. (2 Cor. 6:6)

Just think how much more the blood of Christ will purify our consciences from sinful deeds so that we can worship the living God. For by the power of the eternal Spirit, Christ offered himself to God as a perfect sacrifice for our sins. (Heb. 9:14)

Questions:

1.) Do you feel you have benefited from purity in your life? What is it about purity which is represented in God's word that seems to really impact your life the most?

2.) What does scripture say about purity for the believer (Ps. 19:9; Prov. 20:9; Matt. 5:8; 1 Cor. 1:30; Phil. 4:8; 1 Tim. 5:22; James. 1:27; 1 Pet. 3:2; 2 Pet. 3:14; 1 John 3:3)?

3.) Why is this quality of having purity important to living the providential life?

24. **Integrity** is a quality that incorporates many other attributes of a Christian. Examples of persons with great integrity are found throughout scripture. Notice that persons of integrity are not always connected to fame, fortune, or accomplishments.

Nevertheless, persons with integrity make their mark for their reliance on righteousness.

SCRIPTURAL PROVIDENTIAL INSIGHT

Then the Lord asked Satan, "Have you noticed my servant Job? He is the finest man in all the earth. He is blameless, a man of complete integrity. He fears God and stays away from evil. And he has maintained his integrity, even though you urged me to harm him without cause. (Job 2:3)

May integrity and honesty protect me, for I put my hope in you. (Ps. 25:21)

And you yourself must be an example to them by doing good works of every kind. Let everything you do reflect the integrity and seriousness of your teaching. (Titus 2:7)

Questions:

1.) Do you feel you have benefited from integrity in your life? What is it about the integrity which is represented in God's word that seems to really impact your life the most?

2.) What does scripture say about integrity for the believer (Job 2:9; Job 27:5; Ps. 26:11; Ps. 111:8; Ps. 119:1; Prov. 2:7; 10:9)?

3.) Why is this quality of having integrity that is important to living the providential life?

25. Christians have the **ability to bear adversity** in a world that is inherently unfriendly to them. Throughout the scriptures we see adversity as a factor for those that believed in and followed God. Christ was confronted with adversity as was Noah, Abraham, Isaac, Jacob, Joseph, Moses and many other key figures in the Bible.

SCRIPTURAL PROVIDENTIAL INSIGHT

Moses sent messengers from Kadesh to the king of Edom, "Thus says your brother Israel: You know all the adversity that has befallen us: how our ancestors went down to Egypt, and we lived in Egypt a long time; and the Egyptians oppressed us and our ancestors; and when we cried to the Lord, he heard our voice, and sent an angel and brought us out of Egypt; and here we are in Kadesh, a town on the edge of your territory. (Num. 20:14–16 NRSV)

They think in their heart, "We shall not be moved; throughout all generations we shall not meet adversity." (Ps. 10:6 NRSV)

Questions:

1.) Do you feel you have benefited from the ability to bear adversity in your life? What is it about the ability to bear adversity which is represented in God's word that seems to really impact your life the most?

2.) What does scripture say about the ability to bear adversity for the believer (Deut. 30:15; 2 Sam. 4:9; 1 Kings 1:29; Job 36:15; Prov. 17:17; Eccl. 7:14; Isa. 48:10)?

3.) Why is the ability to bear adversity important to living the providential life?

26. **Fear** of God is a characteristic of a committed Christian. Believers are not to fear what others do but to keep focused upon fear of God and our hope with gentleness and reverence. We are only to fear God with reverence, wonder, awe, worship and obedience.

SCRIPTURAL PROVIDENTIAL INSIGHT

Serve the Lord with reverent fear, and rejoice with trembling. (Ps. 2:11)

I prayed to the Lord, and he answered me. He freed me from all my fears. Ps. 34:4)

So we can say with confidence, "The Lord is my helper, so I will have no fear. What can mere people do to me?" (Heb. 13:6)

Questions:

1.) Do you feel you have benefited from the fear of God and freedom from worldly fear in your life? What is it about fear which is represented in God's word that seems to really impact your life the most?

2.) What does scripture say about the quality of fear for the believer (Deut 6:13; 8:6; Josh. 4:24; 1 Sam. 12:14; Neh. 5:15; Job: 1:8; Ps. 76:7; 2 Cor. 7:1; Rev. 11:18)?

3.) Why is this quality of fear important to living the providential life?

27. The believer in Jesus Christ lives within a **protection and refuge**. The believer can rest in the ultimate protection of Christ because of his complete authority on heaven and earth. This does not mean that no bad things can happen on earth to a believer. It does mean that the believer's ultimate assurance of salvation and eternal life is preserved.

SCRIPTURAL PROVIDENTIAL INSIGHT

The eternal God is your refuge, and his everlasting arms are under you. He drives out the enemy before you; he cries out, "Destroy them!" (Deut. 33:27)

The Lord is my rock, my fortress, and my savior; my God is my rock, in whom I find protection. He is my shield, the power that saves me, and my place of safety. He is my refuge, my savior, the one who saves me from violence. (2 Sam. 22:3)

God is our refuge and strength, always ready to help in times of trouble. (Ps. 46:1)

Questions:

1.) Do you feel you have benefited from the protection and refuge of God in your life? What is it about protection and refuge which is represented in God's word that seems to really impact your life the most?

2) What does scripture say about the quality of refuge and protection for the believer (Gen. 15:1; Num. 6:24; Ps. 27:1; 2 Sam. 22:3; Ps. 71:1; John 17:11)?

3.) Why is this quality of refuge and protection important to living the providential life?

28. The Christian can rely on the quality of **perseverance** to overcome in our tribulations. The believer learns through suffering and rejection in our present world and the hope of the future resurrection and eternal life of the necessity of perseverance. The perseverance of the saints is required for kingdom living.

SCRIPTURAL PROVIDENTIAL INSIGHT

Not only so, but we also glory in our sufferings, because we know that suffering produces perseverance, perseverance, character, and character, hope. And hope does not put us to shame, because God's love has been poured out into our hearts through the Holy Spirit, who has been given to us. (Rom. 5:3–5 NIV)

Rejoice in hope, be patient in suffering, persevere in prayer. (Rom. 12:12 NRSV)

Pursue righteousness and a godly life, along with faith, love, perseverance, and gentleness. (1 Tim. 6:11)

Questions:

1.) Do you feel you have benefited from perseverance in your Christian walk? What is it about perseverance which is represented in God's word that seems to really impact your life the most?

2.) What does scripture say about the quality of perseverance for the believer (Dan. 12:12; Eph. 6:18; Heb. 12:1; Rev. 13:10)?

3.) Why is this quality of perseverance important to living the providential life?

29. The source of **hope** for the believer is found in the Holy Spirit who lives in us. Paul said that any sufferings we endure are not worth comparing to what we will experience in future revelations. Hope is one of the greatest blessings to all Christians. Hope represents a bridge between this life and the eternal life of the future.

Scriptural Providential Insight

And this hope will not lead to disappointment. For we know how dearly God loves us, because he has given us the Holy Spirit to fill our hearts with his love. (Rom. 5:5)

We were given this hope when we were saved. (If we already have something, we don't need to hope for it. But if we look forward to something we don't yet have, we must wait patiently and confidently.) (Rom. 8:24–25)

And all who have this hope in him purify themselves, just as he is pure. (1 John 3:3 NRSV)

Questions:

1.) Do you feel you have benefited from hope in your Christian walk? What is it about hope which is represented in God's word that seems to really impact your life the most?

2.) What does scripture say about the quality of hope for the believer (Rom. 5:4–5; 8:20–21; 15:4; 1 Cor. 15:19; Eph. 2:12; 1 Thess. 1:3; Heb. 10:23; 1 Pet. 3:15)?

3.) Why is this quality of hope important to living the providential life?

30. The wise believer will stand on **noble** things. We are to meditate upon constructive things including those that are noble. Christians that have a noble character are especially blessed. A noble character reflects upon genuine love in a person that exhibits it. A noble quality is one of excellence, high morals and superior ideals.

Scriptural Providential Insight

But those who are noble plan noble things, and by noble things they stand. (Isa. 32:8 NRSV)

From the bed where it was planted it was transplanted to good soil by abundant waters, so that it might produce branches and bear fruit and become a noble vine. (Ezek. 17:7–8 NRSV)

Do not repay anyone evil for evil, but take thought for what is noble in the sight of all. (Rom. 12:17 NRSV)

Questions:

1.) Do you feel you have benefited from the quality of noble pursuits in your Christian walk? What is it about being noble represented in God's word that seems to really impact your life the most?

2.) What does scripture say about the quality of being noble for the believer (Esther: 6:9; Prov. 8:6; Ezek. 17:23; Phil. 4:8)?

3.) Why is this quality of being noble important to living the providential life?

11.3–MY STUDY GUIDE JOURNAL

Personal Reflections on My Study of a Providential Life

Peace

Truth

Purity

Integrity

Ability to Bear Adversity

No Fear

Protection & Refuge

Perseverance

Hope

Noble

31. It is a wonderful quality for believers to **exhort one another**. This is a powerful method of building up the body of Christ. There is a needful urgency in this quality for sustaining and supporting the church. The timing of this quality is important and key to the overall effectiveness of the quality.

SCRIPTURAL PROVIDENTIAL INSIGHT

Exhort bondservants to be obedient to their own masters, to be well pleasing in all *things*, not answering back, not pilfering, but showing all good fidelity, that they may adorn the doctrine of God our Savior in all things. (Titus 2:9–10 NKJV)

But exhort one another every day, as long as it is called "today," so that none of you may be hardened by the deceitfulness of sin. For we have become partners of Christ, if only we hold our first confidence firm to the end. (Heb. 3:13–14 NRSV)

Questions:

1.) Do you feel you have benefited from the quality of exhorting others in your Christian walk? What is it about exhorting one another represented in God's word that seems to really impact your life the most?

2.) What does scripture say about the quality of exhorting others for the believer (Acts 11:23; 15:32; 20:1; 28:15; Rom. 1:12; 12:8; 1 Cor. 8:10; 2 Cor. 7:6; Eph. 6:22; Col. 4:8; 1 Thess. 3:2; 5:11; 1 Pet. 5:12; 2 John 1:11)?

3.) Why is this quality of exhorting others important to living the providential life?

32.   An essential quality of believers is found in **forgiveness**. Our God is a God of forgiveness and we are expected to mirror this characteristic in our own lives so we can also receive forgiveness. The forgiveness of sins by our Savior is paramount to our own salvation. We must forgive others of wrongs they may have committed against us.

SCRIPTURAL PROVIDENTIAL INSIGHT

If you forgive those who sin against you, your heavenly Father will forgive you. But if you refuse to forgive others, your Father will not forgive your sins. (Matt. 6:14–15)

But people are counted as righteous, not because of their work, but because of their faith in God who forgives sinners. (Rom. 4:5)

Make allowance for each other's faults, and forgive anyone who offends you. Remember, the Lord forgave you, so you must forgive others. (Col. 3:13)

Questions:

1.) Do you feel you have benefited from the quality of forgiveness in your Christian walk? What is it about forgiveness represented in God's word that seems to really impact your life the most?

2.) What does scripture say about the quality of forgiveness for the believer (Gen. 50:17; Ps. 79:9; Isa. 55:7; Luke 6:37; 7:47; 11:4; John 20:23; Acts 5:31; 1 John 1:9)?

3.) What is about this quality of forgiveness that is so important to living the providential life?

33. God gives the gift of **purpose** to the believers in Jesus Christ. This quality of purpose resides in the heart of believers by having an overriding purpose until God's plan is complete. Believers are to work together in the universal church to achieve the necessary objectives included in God's plan. The scriptures give us the assurance that all things will work together for those that are called according to His purpose for them (see Rom. 8:28).

SCRIPTURAL PROVIDENTIAL INSIGHT

You can make many plans, but the Lord's purpose will prevail. (Prov. 19:21)

Do not be ashamed, then, of the testimony about our Lord or of me his prisoner, but join with me in suffering for the gospel, relying on the power of God, who saved us and called us with a holy calling, not according to our works but according to his own purpose and grace. (2 Tim. 1:8–9 NRSV)

Questions:

1.) Do you feel you have benefited from the quality of purpose in your Christian walk? What is it about purpose as represented in God's word that seems to really impact your life the most?

2.) What does scripture say about the quality of purpose for the believer (Eccles. 3:1–8; Acts 20:27; Rom. 8:28; 9:11; 1 Cor. 9:26; Phil. 2:2)?

3.) What is it about this quality of purpose that is important to living the providential life?

34. Scripture makes clear that the quality of **patience** should characterize a believer. This quality of patience presents itself in God's key servants throughout the Bible. These servants struggle with patience just as we do today at times. Patience is a feature of coping with trials that strengthens the believer, making them perfect and complete.

SCRIPTURAL PROVIDENTIAL INSIGHT

My brethren, count it all joy when you fall into various trials, knowing that the testing of your faith produces patience. But let patience have *its* perfect work, that you may be perfect and complete, lacking nothing. (James 1:2–4 NKJV).

Rejoice in our confident hope. Be patient in trouble, and keep on praying. (Rom. 12:12)

May God, who gives this patience and encouragement, help you live in complete harmony with each other, as is fitting for followers of Christ Jesus. (Rom. 15:5)

Questions:

1.) Do you feel you have benefited from the quality of patience in your Christian walk? What is it about patience that is represented in God's word that seems to really impact your life the most?

2.) What does scripture say about the quality patience for the believer (Rom. 15:5; Gal. 5:22; Col. 1:11; Col. 3:12; 2 Tim. 3:10; Titus 2:2; James 5:10; 2 Pet. 3:15)?

3.) What is it about this quality of patience that is important to living the providential life?

35. Being a person that is **just** should be a quality of every Christian. We should reflect the perfect justice found in our Father God. A god without justice is not a god worthy of worship. Justice is essential because of the nature of our God. He is perfect in the justice he administers.

SCRIPTURAL PROVIDENTIAL INSIGHT

He is the Rock; his deeds are perfect. Everything he does is just and fair. He is a faithful God who does no wrong; how just and upright he is! (Deut. 32:4)

The plans of the godly are just; the advice of the wicked is treacherous. (Prov. 12:5)

He gives justice to the oppressed and food to the hungry. (Ps. 146:7)

Questions:

1.) Do you feel you have benefited from the quality of justice in your Christian walk? What is it about justice that is represented in God's word that seems to really impact your life the most?

2.) What does scripture say about the quality of justice for the believer (1 Kings 3:11; Job 9:2; Ps. 9:8; 45:7; 99:4; Prov. 29:26; Isa. 42:1; Matt. 5:6; Heb. 1:8; 1 John 1:9; Rev. 19:2)?

3.) What is it about this quality of justice that is important to living the providential life?

36. A Christian believer is a person who should aspire to be **meek**. Few characteristics of a Christian illustrate maturity in the faith more than does this trait. Scripture indicates that this quality is particularly important in defending our faith and witnessing to others. Those that are perceived as "holy" are inevitably blessed with a measure of meekness.

SCRIPTURAL PROVIDENTIAL INSIGHT

But the meek shall inherit the land, and delight themselves in abundant prosperity. (Ps. 37:11 NRSV)

The meek shall obtain fresh joy in the Lord, and the neediest people shall exult in the Holy One of Israel. (Isa. 29:19 NRSV)

Blessed are the meek, for they will inherit the earth. (Matt. 5:5 NRSV)

Questions:

1.) Do you feel you have benefited from the quality of meekness in your Christian walk? What is it about being meek represented in God's word that seems to really impact your life the most?

2.) What does scripture say about the quality of meekness for the believer (Ps. 10:17; Isa. 11:4; Col. 3:12)?

3.) What is it about the quality of meekness that is important to living the providential life?

37. A Christian believer who is clothed with a **humble** quality is exhibiting a Christian quality of special significance. Those with this quality the scriptures teach will be given grace. Scripture also connects those that are humble as also being gentle and meek. We are to especially humble ourselves before God.

SCRIPTURAL PROVIDENTIAL INSIGHT

Though the Lord is great, he cares for the humble, but he keeps his distance from the proud. (Ps. 138:6)

Take my yoke upon you. Let me teach you, because I am humble and gentle at heart, and you will find rest for your souls. (Matt. 11:29)

Finally, all of you should be of one mind. Sympathize with each other. Love each other as brothers and sisters. Be tenderhearted, and keep a humble attitude. (1 Pet. 3:8)

Questions:

1.) Do you feel you have benefited from the quality of humility in your Christian walk? What is it about being humble represented in God's word that seems to really impact your life the most?

2.) What does scripture say about the quality of humility for the believer (Num. 12:3; Ps. 149:4; Zech 9:9; Matt. 5:5; Eph. 4:2; Phil. 2:3; Jas. 4:6; 1 Pet. 5:5)?

3.) What is it about the quality of humility that is important to living the providential life?

38. A classic characteristic of a Christian is the quality of **hospitality**. This is an important quality that Christ put a high value upon in evaluating people at final judgment (see Matt. 25:38). The Bible features the significance of hospitality throughout scripture. One of the first and finest examples of hospitality in the Bible is found in Genesis 18.

SCRIPTURAL PROVIDENTIAL INSIGHT

When God's people are in need, be ready to help them. Always be eager to practice hospitality. (Rom. 12:13)

Then those righteous ones will reply, 'Lord, when did we ever see you hungry and feed you? Or thirsty and give you something to drink? Or a stranger and show you hospitality? Or naked and give you clothing? When did we ever see you sick or in prison and visit you?' "And the King will say, 'I tell you the truth, when you did it to one of the least of these my brothers and sisters, you were doing it to me!'" (Matt. 25:37–40)

Questions:

1.) Do you feel you have benefited from the quality of hospitality in your Christian walk? What is it about being hospitable represented in God's word that seems to really impact your life the most?

2.) What does scripture say about the quality of hospitality for the believer (Gen. 18:1–8; Luke 10:7; 1 Tim. 5:10; Heb. 13:2)?

3.) What is it about the quality of hospitality that is important to living the providential life?

39. A Christian should possess the quality of being **gracious**. A person who is gracious possesses kindness, mercy and compassion. Christ was the supreme example of this characteristic. We can see this example through God the Father in the Old Testament and in Christ found in the New Testament.

SCRIPTURAL PROVIDENTIAL INSIGHT

May the Lord bless you and protect you. May the Lord smile on you and be gracious to you. May the Lord show you his favor and give you his peace. (Num. 6:24–26)

For your kingdom is an everlasting kingdom. You rule throughout all generations. The Lord always keeps his promises; he is gracious in all he does. (Ps. 145:13)

Gracious is the Lord, and righteous; our God is merciful. (Ps. 116:5 NRSV)

Questions:

1.) Do you feel you have benefited from the quality of graciousness in your Christian walk? What is it about being gracious represented in God's word that seems to really impact your life the most?

2.) What does scripture say about the quality of being gracious for the believer (2 Kings 13:23; Prov. 11:16; John 1:16; 2 Cor. 8:7; Col. 4:6; 1 Tim. 1:14; 1 Pet. 1:10)?

3.) What is it about the quality of being gracious that is important to living the providential life?

40. A natural quality of a mature Christian is **understanding**. Christ gave the quality of understanding a whole new dimension for believers. At the same time we must remember that some spiritual concepts defy any efforts of our understanding (see Phil. 4:7).

SCRIPTURAL PROVIDENTIAL INSIGHT

I will pursue your commands, for you expand my understanding. (Ps. 119:32)

The wise are known for their understanding, and pleasant words are persuasive. (Prov. 16:21)

And I know it is important to love him with all my heart and all my understanding and all my strength, and to love my neighbor as myself. (Mark 12:33)

Questions:

1.) Do you feel you have benefited from the quality of understanding in your Christian walk? What is it about understanding represented in God's word that seems to really impact your life the most?

2.) What does scripture say about the quality of understanding for the believer (Job 28:28; Ps. 119:34; Prov. 14:29; 18:2; 19:8; 20:5; Isa. 50:4; Luke 2:47; 1 Cor. 14:20; Eph 1:8)?

3.) What is it about the quality of understanding that is important to living the providential life?

11.4 My Study Guide Journal

Personal Reflections on My Study of a Providential Life

Exhort One Another

Forgiveness

Purpose

Patience

Just

Meek

Humble

Hospitality

Gracious

Understanding

41. A necessary quality of a Christian is **care**. Christ exhibited care in his ministry with unrelenting detail. One could easily say that this was the hallmark of Christ's mission. He cared for humans more than anyone who ever lived. We are to continue this care in the world as believers in our Lord and Savior.

SCRIPTURAL PROVIDENTIAL INSIGHT

And you saw how the Lord your God cared for you all along the way as you traveled through the wilderness, just as a father cares for his child. Now he has brought you to this place. (Deut. 1:31)

I was naked, and you gave me clothing. I was sick, and you cared for me. I was in prison, and you visited me. (Matt. 25:36)

Care for the flock that God has entrusted to you. Watch over it willingly, not grudgingly, not for what you will get out of it, but because you are eager to serve God. (1 Pet. 5:2)

Questions:

1.) Do you feel you have benefited from the quality of care in your Christian walk? What is it about care represented in God's word that seems to really impact your life the most?

2.) What does scripture say about the quality of care for the believer (Ps. 8:4; 37:17; 65:9; 138:6; Prov. 12:10; Isa. 53:8; Matt. 6:30; John 10:13; Eph. 5:29; 1 Pet. 5:7)?

3.) What is it about the quality of care that is important to living the providential life?

42. A quality of a believer that indicates an established Christian is **gentleness**. The Bible gives great due to the power of the tongue. It can be a powerful force for good and a negative force in a person's life. We can strengthen our Christian impact in the world through gentleness.

SCRIPTURAL PROVIDENTIAL INSIGHT

Gentle words are a tree of life; a deceitful tongue crushes the spirit. (Prov. 15:4)

Which do you choose? Should I come with a rod to punish you, or should I come with love and a gentle spirit? (1Cor. 4:21)

> They must not slander anyone and must avoid quarreling. Instead, they should
> be gentle and show true humility to everyone. (Titus 3:2)

Questions:

1.) Do you feel you have benefited from the quality of gentleness in your Christian walk? What is it about gentleness represented in God's word that seems to really impact your life the most?

2.) What does scripture say about the quality of gentleness for the believer (1 Kings 19:12; Prov. 15:1; Gal. 5:23; Eph. 4:2; Col. 3:12; 1 Tim. 3:3; James 3:17)?

3.) What is it about the quality of gentleness that is important to living the providential life?

43. A mature believer is known for their quality of **reverence** (see Job 37:24). This is a characteristic that incorporates many other areas of Christian qualities. However, it could be said that many of these in this case rest upon the ideas of admiration, respect, veneration and awe of the object of our worship and source of life.

Scriptural Providential Insight

> But as for me, by Your abundant lovingkindness I will enter Your house, At
> Your holy temple I will bow in reverence for You. (Ps. 5:7 NASB)

> Therefore, since we have these promises, dear friends, let us purify ourselves
> from everything that contaminates body and spirit, perfecting holiness out of
> reverence for God. (2 Cor. 7:1 NIV)

Questions:

1.) Do you feel you have benefited from the quality of reverence in your Christian walk? What is it about reverence represented in God's word that seems to really impact your life the most?

2.) What does scripture say about the quality of reverence for the believer (Lev. 19:30; Job 15:4; 37:24; Eph. 5:21; Col. 3:22; Heb. 5:7; 1 Pet. 1:17; 3:2)?

3.) What is it about the quality of reverence that is important to living the providential life?

44. The quality of **mercy** is certainly one that reflects Christ's example. God has displayed mercy on humans throughout history. We should show this same mercy upon others as we received from Christ. Christ challenged us to learn the meaning of showing mercy (see Matt. 9:13).

Scriptural Providential Insight

"I'm in a desperate situation!" David replied to Gad. "But let us fall into the hands of the Lord, for his mercy is great. Do not let us fall into human hands." (2 Sam. 24:14)

"O my God, lean down and listen to me. Open your eyes and see our despair. See how your city, the city that bears your name, lies in ruins. We make this plea, not because we deserve help, but because of your mercy." (Daniel 9:18)

"And you must show mercy to those whose mercy is wavering." (Jude 1:22)

Questions:

1.) Do you feel you have benefited from the quality of mercy in your Christian walk? What is it about mercy represented in God's word that seems to really impact your life the most?

2.) What does scripture say about the quality of mercy for the believer (Exod. 34:6; Neh. 9:27; Job 41:3; Ps. 103:4; Isa. 14:1; Matt. 5:7; Rom. 9:15; 11:32; Gal. 1:6)?

3.) What is it about the quality of mercy that is important to living the providential life?

45. **Kindness** is not least in the qualities of the Christian. Common sense dictates to the believer that they should reflect the incredible kindness that Christ exhibited throughout his life on this earth. Kindness will reward the believer in so many ways as an expression of Christ's love in this world.

Scriptural Providential Insight

If your gift is to encourage others, be encouraging. If it is giving, give generously. If God has given you leadership ability, take the responsibility seriously. And if you have a gift for showing kindness to others, do it gladly. (Rom. 12:8)

But the Holy Spirit produces this kind of fruit in our lives: love, joy, peace, patience, kindness, goodness, faithfulness, gentleness, and self-control. There is no law against these things! (Gal. 5:22)

Like newborn babies, you must crave pure spiritual milk so that you will grow into a full experience of salvation. Cry out for this nourishment, now that you have had a taste of the Lord's kindness. (1 Pet. 2:2–3)

Questions:

1.) Do you feel you have benefited from the quality of kindness in your Christian walk? What is it about kindness represented in God's word that seems to really impact your life the most?

2.) What does scripture say about the quality of kindness for the believer (Ps. 106:7; Rom. 2:4; 2 Cor. 6:1; 8:1; 10:1; Eph. 2:7; Col. 3:12; Titus 3:4)?

3.) What is it about the quality of kindness that is important to living the providential life?

46. The providence of God is powerful and complete when we **trust** in our Lord. This is an essential and foundational feature of human salvation. Jesus explained the tremendous importance of trust. The power of this trust gives us hope for eternity with God in heaven.

Scriptural Providential Insight

He has given me a new song to sing, a hymn of praise to our God. Many will see what he has done and be amazed. They will put their trust in the Lord. (Ps. 40:3)

I have come as a light to shine in this dark world, so that all who put their trust in me will no longer remain in the dark. (John 12:46)

So now Jesus and the ones he makes holy have the same Father. That is why Jesus is not ashamed to call them his brothers and sisters. For he said to God. "I will proclaim your name to my brothers and sisters. I will praise you among your assembled people." He also said, "I will put my trust in him," that is, "I and the children God has given me." (Heb. 2:11–13)

Questions:

1.) Do you feel you have benefited from the quality of trust in your Christian walk? What is it about trust represented in God's word that seems to really impact your life the most?

2.) What does scripture say about the quality of trust for the believer (1 Chron. 5:20; Ps. 56:3; Isa. 2:22; Jer. 13:25; Matt. 18:6; John 2:24; 12:44; 14:1; Rom. 9:33; 15:13; Phil. 1:29)?

3.) What is it about the quality of trust that is important to living the providential life?

47. A believer has a soul that shall **abide** in well–being (see Ps. 25:13). The quality of abiding in Christ is a unique concept that is basic to the light and life represented by our Savior. The disciples of Christ abide in his word (see John 8:31).

SCRIPTURAL PROVIDENTIAL INSIGHT

So Jesus said to the Jews who had believed in him, "If you abide in my word, you are my disciples, and you will know the truth, and the truth will set you free." (John 8:31 ESV)

Abide in me, and I in you. As the branch cannot bear fruit by itself, unless it abides in the vine, neither can you, unless you abide in me. I am the vine; you are the branches. Whoever abides in me and I in him, he it is that bears much fruit, for apart from me you can do nothing. If anyone does not abide in me he is thrown away like a branch and withers; and the branches are gathered, thrown into the fire and burned. (John 15:4–6 ESV)

As the Father has loved me, so have I loved you. Abide in my love. If you keep my commandments you will abide in my love, just as I have kept my Father's commandments and abide in his love. (John 15:9–10 ESV)

Questions:

1.) Do you feel you have benefited from the quality of abide in your Christian walk? What is it about the concept of abide represented in God's word that seems to really impact your life the most?

2.) What does scripture say about the quality of abide for the believer (Ps. 25:13; 125:1; Is. 32:16; 1 John 2:28; 4:13; 2 John 9)?

3.) What is it about the quality of abide that is important to living the providential life?

48. A believer who stands strong in the faith and wisdom of Jesus Christ is considered to be **mature**. Paul encouraged believers to grow to maturity (see 2 Cor. 13:11). This quality is a combination of most other Christian characteristics. It is this joining of qualities that prepares the believer for witnessing to others and eventually for eternal life.

SCRIPTURAL PROVIDENTIAL INSIGHT

Dear brothers and sisters, I close my letter with these last words: Be joyful. Grow to maturity. Encourage each other. Live in harmony and peace. Then the God of love and peace will be with you. (2 Cor. 13:11)

This will continue until we all come to such unity in our faith and knowledge of God's Son that we will be mature in the Lord, measuring up to the full and complete standard of Christ. (Eph. 4:13)

I am writing to you who are mature in the faith because you know Christ, who existed from the beginning. (1 John 2:13)

Questions:

1.) Do you feel you have benefited from the quality of maturity in your Christian walk? What is it about maturity represented in God's word that seems to really impact your life the most?

2.) What does scripture say about the quality of maturity for the believer (Luke 8:14; 1 Cor. 2:6; 14:20; 2 Cor. 13:9; Phil. 3:15; Heb. 6:1; 1 John 2:13)?

3.) What is it about the quality of maturity that is important to living the providential life?

49. The quality of any believer must include that quality of being able to **listen**. Otherwise, how can they receive the Word of God? The ability to listen is a critical factor for any believer as described in scripture. We receive God's instructions and providential plan by listening.

SCRIPTURAL PROVIDENTIAL INSIGHT

Listen closely, Israel, and be careful to obey. Then all will go well with you, and you will have many children in the land flowing with milk and honey, just as the Lord, the God of your ancestors, promised you. (Deut. 6:3)

Fools think their own way is right, but the wise listen to others. (Prov. 12:15)

My sheep listen to my voice. I know them, and they follow me. (John 10:27)

Understand this, my dear brothers and sisters: You must all be quick to listen, slow to speak, and slow to get angry. (James 1:19)

Questions:

1.) Do you feel you have benefited from the quality of listening in your Christian walk? What is it about listening represented in God's word that seems to really impact your life the most?

2.) What does Scripture say about the quality of listening for the believer (Neh. 8:3; Ps. 95:7; Isa. 6:9; Dan. 9:6; Mark 9:7; Luke 16:31; John 15:20; 1 Tim. 2:12; 1 John 4:6; Rev. 2:7)?

3.) What is it about the quality of listening that is important to living the providential life?

50. **Forgiveness** is a quality Christ demands of the believer. Christ set the standard of this character quality that we must share with our fellow human. We all need forgiveness from Jesus Christ and from our fellow brother and sister. We have all sinned and come short of the standard of Christ and as a result require forgiveness.

SCRIPTURAL PROVIDENTIAL INSIGHT

The Lord said, "I will pardon them as you have requested. But as surely as I live, and as surely as the earth is filled with the Lord's glory, not one of these people will ever enter that land." (Num. 14:20–22)

Help us, O God of our salvation! Help us for the glory of your name. Save us and forgive our sins for the honor of your name. (Ps. 79:9)

So I will prove to you that the Son of Man has the authority on earth to forgive sins. (Matt. 9:6)

Then God put him in the place of honor at his right hand as Prince and Savior. He did this so the people of Israel would repent of their sins and be forgiven. (Acts 5:31)

Questions:

1.) Do you feel you have benefited from the quality of forgiveness in your Christian walk? What is it about forgiveness represented in God's word that seems to really impact your life the most?

2.) What does scripture say about the quality of forgiveness for the believer (Exod. 34:7; 1 Kings 8:34; Prov. 17:9; Jer. 31:34; Matt. 6:14; Mark 11:25; Acts 8:22; Rom. 4:7)?

3.) What is it about the quality of forgiveness that is important to living the providential life?

11.5–My Study Guide Journal

Personal Reflections on My Study of a Providential Life

Care	**Trust**
Gentleness	**Abide**
Reverence	**Maturity**
Mercy	**Listen**
Kindness	**Forgiveness**

51. God provides us with the grace of **confession**. We are encouraged throughout the pages of scripture to confess our transgressions to God. This is essential for a follower of God and Jesus Christ. We must confess just like we repent of our sins.

SCRIPTURAL PROVIDENTIAL INSIGHT

But I confess my sins; I am deeply sorry for what I have done. (Ps. 38:18)

Come and listen, all you who fear God, and I will tell you what he did for me. For I cried out to him for help, praising him as I spoke. If I had not confessed the sin in my heart, the Lord would not have listened. But God did listen! He paid attention to my prayer. Praise God, who did not ignore my prayer or withdraw his unfailing love from me. (Ps. 66:16–20)

And when they confessed their sins, he baptized them in the Jordan River. (Mark 1:5b)

Questions:

1.) Do you feel you have benefited from the quality of confession in your Christian walk? What is it about confession represented in God's word that seems to really impact your life the most?

2.) What does scripture say about the quality of confession for the believer (1 Sam. 7:6; Ezra 10:11; Ps. 32:3; 38:18; 66:18; Dan. 9:4; Matt. 18:15; James 5:16; 1 John 1:9)?

3.) What is it about the quality of confession that is important to living the providential life?

52. The quality of **joy** is truly one of distinction and treasure for the Christian believer. The word "joy" is mentioned well over two hundred times in scripture covering over half of the books of the Bible. Although the people of God suffered and were persecuted at times throughout the scriptures, joy is certainly a characteristic associated with God and Jesus Christ.

SCRIPTURAL PROVIDENTIAL INSIGHT

When the victorious Israelite army was returning home after David had killed the Philistine, women from all the towns of Israel came out to meet King Saul. They sang and danced for joy with tambourines and cymbals. (1 Sam. 18:6)

So everyone who had returned from captivity lived in these shelters during the festival, and they were all filled with great joy! (Neh. 8:17)

You haven't done this before. Ask, using my name, and you will receive, and you will have abundant joy. (John 16:24)

Questions:

1.) Do you feel you have benefited from the quality of joy in your Christian walk? What is it about joy represented in God's word that seems to really impact your life the most?

2.) What does scripture say about the quality of joy for the believer (Deut. 16:15; Ps. 1:1; 28:7; 41:1; 65:8; Prov. 21:15; Isa. 12:6; Matt. 2:10; Luke 10:21; John 16:20; Phil. 4:1)?

3.) What is it about the quality of joy that is important to living the providential life?

53. A quality common to all Christian believers is that they have **believed** in Jesus Christ as their Savior. The importance of the act of believing and belief is emphasized in the New Testament. Belief in Christ is our fundamental duty in receiving the gift of salvation.

Scriptural Providential Insight

What do you mean, "If I can?" Jesus asked. "Anything is possible if a person believes." (Mark 9:23)

Then Jesus said to them, "You foolish people! You find it so hard to believe all that the prophets wrote in the Scriptures. Wasn't it clearly predicted that the Messiah would have to suffer all these things before entering his glory?" (Luke 24:25–26)

We are made right with God by placing our faith in Jesus Christ. And this is true for everyone who believes, no matter who we are. (Rom. 3:22)

Questions:

1.) Do you feel you have benefited from the quality of belief in your Christian walk? What is it about belief represented in God's word that seems to really impact your life the most?

2.) What does scripture say about the quality of belief for the believer (Gen. 15:6; Matt. 27:42; Mark 15:32; John 3:16; 7:39; 11:40; 13:19; Rom. 10:9; 2 Cor. 5:7; Heb. 3:14; 1 John 5:10)?

3.) What is it about the quality of belief that is important to living the providential life?

54. **Self–control** is an important quality of a Christian. This characteristic is a result of many other Christian qualities and their influence upon the believer. Self–control is a quality that is especially evident in the mature and older Christian (see Titus 2:2). As we release our control to that of Christ in our lives this quality becomes more relevant.

Scriptural Providential Insight

For the Lord sees clearly what a man does, examining every path he takes. An evil man is held captive by his own sins; they are ropes that catch and hold him. He will die for lack of self–control; he will be lost because of his great foolishness. (Prov. 5:21–23)

As he reasoned with them about righteousness and self–control and the coming day of judgment, Felix became frightened. (Acts 24:25)

So prepare your minds for action and exercise self–control. Put all your hope in the gracious salvation that will come to you when Jesus Christ is revealed to the world. (1 Pet. 1:13)

Questions:

1.) Do you feel you have benefited from the quality of self–control in your Christian walk? What is it about self–control represented in God's word that seems to really impact your life the most?

2.) What does scripture say about the quality of self–control for the believer (Prov. 16:32; Gal. 5:22–23; 1 Tim. 3:2,11; Titus 2:2; 2 Pet. 1:6)?

3.) What is it about the quality of self–control that is important to living the providential life?

55. The believer is referred to as **godly** in many locations throughout the Bible. A believer with true godliness and contentment is a source of great wealth (see 1 Tim. 6:6). Scripture records that some believers described as godly can facilitate miracles (see Acts 22:12–13).

SCRIPTURAL PROVIDENTIAL INSIGHT

A man named Ananias lived there. He was a godly man, deeply devoted to the law, and well regarded by all the Jews of Damascus. He came and stood beside me and said, 'Brother Saul, regain your sight.' And that very moment I could see him! (Acts 22:12–13)

Dear brothers and sisters, if another believer is overcome by some sin, you who are godly should gently and humbly help that person back onto the right path. And be careful not to fall into the same temptation yourself. (Gal. 6:1)

Teach these things, Timothy, and encourage everyone to obey them. Some people may contradict our teaching, but these are the wholesome teachings of the Lord Jesus Christ. These teachings promote a godly life. (1 Tim. 6:2b–3)

Questions:

1.) Do you feel you have benefited from godliness in your Christian walk? What is it about godliness as represented in God's word that seems to really impact your life the most?

2.) What does scripture say about the quality of godliness for the believer (Ps. 31:23; Prov. 16:31; Acts 22:12; Gal. 6:1; 1 Tim. 4:8; 6:3; 6:6; Titus 1:1; 2 Pet. 2:9, 3:11)?

3.) What is it about the quality of godliness that is important to living the providential life?

56. A Christian observes the practice of **rest**. Jesus offers those who believe in him rest. The Christian will also experience a "sabbath" rest or a special rest in the future. This will be a type of rest that parallels that of God after the creation (see Heb. 4:8–11). Rest is a critical feature for the believer, now and in the future.

SCRIPTURAL PROVIDENTIAL INSIGHT

This is what the Sovereign Lord, the Holy One of Israel, says: "Only in returning to me and resting in me will you be saved." (Isa. 30:15)

Then Jesus said, "Come to me, all of you who are weary and carry heavy burdens, and I will give you rest. Take my yoke upon you. Let me teach you, because I am humble and gentle at heart, and you will find rest for your souls. For my yoke is easy to bear, and the burden I give you is light. (Matt. 11:28–30)

And God will provide rest for you who are being persecuted and also for us when the Lord Jesus appears from heaven. He will come with his mighty angels. (2 Thess. 1:7)

Questions:

1.) Do you feel you have benefited from the quality of rest in your Christian walk? What is it about rest represented in God's word that seems to really impact your life the most?

2.) What does scripture say about the quality of rest for the believer (Ps. 91:1; 127:2; Jer. 6:16; Heb. 4:3–4, 9–11; Rev. 14:13)?

3.) What is it about the quality of rest that is important to living the providential life?

57. God will provide the believer **satisfaction** in this life and the next. The satisfaction of a Christian is different than the usual interpretation of the word. Christian satisfaction goes deep, all the way to the level of the soul. This satisfaction has nothing to do with riches or possessions in this world (see James 5:1–5).

SCRIPTURAL PROVIDENTIAL INSIGHT

O God, I beg two favors from you; let me have them before I die. First, help me never to tell a lie. Second, give me neither poverty nor riches! Give me just enough to satisfy my needs. (Prov. 30:7

Then Jesus turned to his disciples and said, "God blesses you who are poor, for the Kingdom of God is yours. God blesses you who are hungry now, for you will be satisfied. God blesses you who weep now, for in due time you will laugh." (Luke 6:20–21)

Don't love money; be satisfied with what you have. For God has said, "I will never fail you. I will never abandon you." (Heb. 13:5)

Questions:

1.) Do you feel you have benefited from the quality of satisfaction in your Christian walk? What is it about satisfaction represented in God's word that seems to really impact your life the most?

2.) What does scripture say about the quality of satisfaction for the believer (Ps. 103:1–5, 107:1–9; Jer. 31:14; Isa. 53:10–11; John 1:16; Eph. 3:18–19; Phil. 4:18–19)?

3.) What is it about the quality of satisfaction that is important to living the providential life?

58. A believer has the quality of being **content** in their life. Christ and the early Christian disciples were content in their lives despite their very modest material possessions. The contentment in the Christian's life is a key strength that allows a more blessed life. We see just the opposite in the world's mantra of today which encourages one to always have more and never be satisfied.

SCRIPTURAL PROVIDENTIAL INSIGHT

Not that I was ever in need, for I have learned how to be content with whatever I have. (Phil. 4:11)

Yet true godliness with contentment is itself great wealth. After all, we brought nothing with us when we came into this world, and we can't take anything with us when we leave it. So if we have enough food and clothing, let us be content. (1 Tim. 6:6–8)

Questions:

1.) Do you feel you have benefited from the quality of being content in your Christian walk? What is it about being content represented in God's word that seems to really impact your life the most?

2.) What does scripture say about the quality of being content for the believer (Josh. 7:7; 1 Kings 4:20; Prov. 13:25; Luke 3:14; Heb. 13:5)?

3.) What is it about the quality of being content that is important to living the providential life?

59. A believer in Jesus Christ gives **thanks** to God and all that he provides. A person who has come to Jesus Christ as their Lord and Savior has much to be thankful. We are encouraged to give thanks for everything in Christ's name to God the Father (see Col. 3:15–17).

SCRIPTURAL PROVIDENTIAL INSIGHT

All of your works will thank you, Lord, and your faithful followers will praise you. (Ps. 145:10)

I urge you, first of all, to pray for all people. Ask God to help them; intercede on their behalf, and give thanks for them. (1 Tim. 2:1)

Since we are receiving a kingdom that is unshakable, let us be thankful and please God by worshiping him with holy fear and awe. (Heb. 12:28)

Questions:

1.) Do you feel you have benefited from the quality of thanks in your Christian walk? What is it about thanks represented in God's word that seems to really impact your life the most?

2.) What does scripture say about the quality of thanks for the believer (Ps. 30:12; 107:1; Rom. 1:21; 1 Cor. 11:24; Phil. 1:3; 1 Tim. 4:3: Rev. 4:9)?

3.) What is it about the quality of thanks that is important to living the providential life?

60. Perhaps the most hallmark quality of a believer should be **love**. The word translated as love appears almost six hundred times in the scriptures. This quality holds special significance because of the application it has to the nature of God and the children of God. A believer should reflect this quality as this is commanded by Christ.

SCRIPTURAL PROVIDENTIAL INSIGHT

I will also bless the foreigners who commit themselves to the Lord, who serve him and love his name, who worship him and do not desecrate the Sabbath day of rest, and who hold fast to my covenant. (Isa. 56:6)

The Father loves his Son and has put everything into his hands. And anyone who believes in God's Son has eternal life. Anyone who doesn't obey the Son will never experience eternal life but remains under God's angry judgment. (John 3:35–36)

Everyone who believes that Jesus is the Christ has become a child of God. And everyone who loves the Father loves his children, too. We know we love God's children if we love God and obey his commandments. Loving God means keeping his commandments, and his commandments are not burdensome. (1 John 5:1–3)

Questions:

1.) Do you feel you have benefited from the quality of love in your Christian walk? What is it about love represented in God's word that seems to really impact your life the most?

2.) What does scripture say about the quality of love for the believer (Gen. 29:32; Deut. 30:16; Ps. 89:28; Matt. 19:19; Luke 10:27; Mark 12:33; John 17:23; 1 John 4:7–8)?

3.) What is it about the quality of love that is important to living the providential life?

11.6–MY STUDY GUIDE JOURNAL

Personal Reflections on My Study of a Providential Life

Confession

Joy

Belief

Self-Control

Godly

Rest

Satisfaction

Content

Thanks

Love

61. A believer of Jesus Christ is providentially **called** of God. This is a critical quality of the believer. God works in ways only He can comprehend in the calling of one to Himself. Examples like Isaac, Jacob and Joseph illustrate how the hand of God works in unusual and unpredictable ways to insure that His will is done.

SCRIPTURAL PROVIDENTIAL INSIGHT

Then if my people who are called by my name will humble themselves and pray and seek my face and turn from their wicked ways, I will hear from heaven and will forgive their sins and restore their land. (2 Chron. 7:14)

This promise is to you, to your children, and to those far away, all who have been called by the Lord our God. (Acts 2:39)

For God's gifts and his call can never be withdrawn. (Rom. 11:29)

So dear brothers and sisters, work hard to prove that you really are among those God has called and chosen. Do these things, and you will never fall away. Then God will give you a grand entrance into the eternal kingdom of our Lord and Savior Jesus Christ. (2 Pet. 1:10–11)

Questions:

1.) Do you feel you have benefited from the quality of being called in your Christian walk? What is it about being called represented in God's word that seems to really impact your life the most?

2.) What does scripture say about the quality of being called (Matt. 2:15; Mark 2:17; Rom. 1:6; 8:28; 1 Cor. 1:24; Gal. 5:13; 1 Thess. 4:7; Heb. 9:15; 2 Pet. 1:10)?

3.) What is it about the quality of being called that is important to living the providential life?

62. A believer of Jesus Christ **belongs** to God and listens gladly to His words. We need to understand that the act of belonging is part of the design God has for those He has called to be children of God. Those that do not belong to God do not hear. This is an essential characteristic of believers.

SCRIPTURAL PROVIDENTIAL INSIGHT

Anyone who belongs to God listens gladly to the words of God. But you don't listen because you don't belong to God. (John 8:47)

The world would love you as one of its own if you belonged to it, but you are no longer part of the world. I chose you to come out of the world, so it hates you. (John 15:19)

Those who belong to Christ Jesus have nailed the passions and desires of their sinful nature to his cross and crucified them there. (Gal. 5:24)

But God's truth stands firm like a foundation stone with this inscription: "The Lord knows those who are his," and "All who belong to the Lord must turn away from evil." (2 Tim. 2:19)

Questions:

1.) Do you feel you have benefited from the quality of belonging in your Christian walk? What is it about belonging represented in God's word that seems to really impact your life the most?

2.) What does scripture say about the quality of belonging for the believer (Lev. 25:55; Rom. 1:6; 12:5; 2 Cor. 10:7; 1 Thess. 5:5; 1 Pet. 3:16; 1 John 4:6)?

3.) What is it about the quality of belonging that is important to living the providential life?

63. A believer of Jesus Christ is **adopted** as a child of God. As a child of God we are adopted as one of God's children, as one of His co-heirs. As adopted children of God we can look forward to a day that is free of evil, death and destruction. How precious is this adopted status to the believer in Christ.

SCRIPTURAL PROVIDENTIAL INSIGHT

So you have not received a spirit that makes you fearful slaves. Instead, you received God's Spirit when he adopted you as his own children. Now we call him "Abba, Father." For his Spirit joins with our spirit to affirm that we are God's children. And since we are his children, we are his heirs. In fact, together with Christ we are heirs of God's glory. But if we are to share his glory, we must also share his suffering. (Roman 8:15–17)

But when the right time came, God sent his Son, born of a woman, subject to the law. God sent him to buy freedom for us who were slaves to the law, so that he could adopt us as his very own children. (Gal. 4:4–5)

Questions:

1.) Do you feel you have benefited from the quality of adoption in your Christian walk? What is it about adoption represented in God's word that seems to really impact your life the most?

2.) What does scripture say about the quality of adoption for the believer (Isa. 44:5; Rom. 8:23; 9:4; Eph. 1:5)?

3.) What is it about the quality of adoption that is important to living the providential life?

64. The Christian believer is a **citizen** of heaven according to Scripture. Citizenship was very important in the time of Christ and Paul. Various rights and privileges were assigned based upon a person's citizenship. It is no different in being a citizen of heaven.

SCRIPTURAL PROVIDENTIAL INSIGHT

So now you Gentiles are no longer strangers and foreigners. You are citizens along with all of God's holy people. You are members of God's family. Together, we are his house, built on the foundation of the apostles and the prophets. And the cornerstone is Christ Jesus himself. (Eph. 2:19–20)

But we are citizens of heaven, where the Lord Jesus Christ lives. And we are eagerly waiting for him to return as our Savior. He will take our weak mortal bodies and change them into glorious bodies like his own, using the same power with which he will bring everything under his control. (Phil. 3:20–21)

Questions:

1.) Do you feel you have benefited from the quality of citizenship in your Christian walk? What is it about citizenship represented in God's word that seems to really impact your life the most?

2.) What does scripture say about the quality of citizenship for the believer (Lev. 16:29; Josh. 8:33; 24:11; Luke 19:14; Acts 16:37; 19:35; Eph. 2:12,19; Phil. 3:20)?

3.) What is it about the quality of citizenship that is important to living the providential life?

65. Believers are **chosen** out of this world by Jesus Christ. The Christian believer has been chosen and destined by God the Father, sanctified by the Spirit and obedient to Jesus Christ (see 1 Pet. 1:2). God chooses His followers not only to insure forgiveness and eternal life, but so that the person can be fruitful and productive to carry out God's purpose.

SCRIPTURAL PROVIDENTIAL INSIGHT

For many are called, but few are chosen. (Matt. 22:14)

You didn't choose me. I chose you. I appointed you to go and produce lasting fruit, so that the Father will give you whatever you ask for, using my name. (John 15:16)

But before they were born, before they had done anything good or bad, she received a message from God. (This message shows that God chooses people according to his own purposes; he calls people, but not according to their good or bad works.) (Rom. 9:11–12a)

Questions:

1.) Do you feel you have benefited from the quality of chosen in your Christian walk? What is it about chosen represented in God's word that seems to really impact your life the most?

2.) What does scripture say about the quality of chosen for the believer (Deut. 30:19; Josh. 24:15; Eccles. 10:2; Jer. 27:5; Dan. 4:25; Rom. 9:18; 1 Pet. 1:2)?

3.) What is it about the quality of chosen that is important to living the providential life?

66. Christ has made it possible for humans to be **reconciled** to Him and given the believer the ministry of reconciliation. As a follower of Jesus we are understanding of the reconciliation that has occurred in the new relationship we enjoy with God. The blood of Christ has made possible for humans to be reconciled to Him.

SCRIPTURAL PROVIDENTIAL INSIGHT

For if while we were enemies we were reconciled to God by the death of his Son, much more, now that we are reconciled, shall we be saved by his life. More than that, we also rejoice in God through our Lord Jesus Christ, through whom we have now received reconciliation. (Rom. 5:10–11 ESV)

And all of this is a gift from God, who brought us back to himself through Christ. And God has given us this task of reconciling people to him. For God was in Christ, reconciling the world to himself, no longer counting people's sins against them. And he gave us this wonderful message of reconciliation. (2 Cor. 5:18–19)

Questions:

1.) Do you feel you have benefited from the quality of being reconciled in your Christian walk? What is it about being reconciled represented in God's word that seems to really impact your life the most?

2.) What does scripture say about the quality of being reconciled for the believer (Prov. 14:9; 2 Cor. 5:18–19; Eph. 2:16; Col. 1:20, 22)?

3.) What is it about the quality of being reconciled that is important to living the providential life?

67. Followers of Jesus Christ are made **blameless** in the sight of God. A Christian is encouraged in scripture to become pure and blameless (see 2 Pet. 3:14). We can only become blameless through our Lord and Savior Jesus Christ. He took upon Himself the blame that we all deserve.

SCRIPTURAL PROVIDENTIAL INSIGHT

He will keep you strong to the end so that you will be free from all blame on the day when our Lord Jesus Christ returns. God will do this, for he is faithful to do what he says, and he has invited you into partnership with his Son, Jesus Christ our Lord. (1 Cor. 1:8–9)

For I want you to understand what really matters, so that you may live pure and blameless lives until the day of Christ's return. (Phil. 1:10)

Now may the God of peace make you holy in every way, and may your whole spirit and soul and body be kept blameless until our Lord Jesus Christ comes again. (1 Thess. 5:23)

Questions:

1.) Do you feel you have benefited from the quality of being blameless in your Christian walk? What is it about being blameless represented in God's word that seems to really impact your life the most?

2.) What does scripture say about the quality of being blameless for the believer (Gen. 6:9; Job 1:8; Ps. 18:23; Prov. 13:6; Col. 1:22; Titus 1:6; 2 Pet. 3:14; Rev. 14:5)?

3.) What is it about the quality of being blameless that is important to living the providential life?

68. A believer is **committed** to Jesus Christ. We are to commit everything in our life to Christ. He doesn't want just part of our commitment. He demands a total commitment. We need to constantly remember this in everything we do. Our trust and commitment to Christ will be repaid a million times over.

SCRIPTURAL PROVIDENTIAL INSIGHT

Commit everything you do to the Lord. Trust him, and he will help you. He will make your innocence radiate like the dawn, and the justice of your cause will shine like the noonday sun. (Ps. 37:5–6)

Jesus answered them, "Truly, truly, I say to you, everyone who commits sin is a slave to sin." (John 8:34 ESV)

He gave his life to free us from every kind of sin, to cleanse us, and to make us his very own people, totally committed to doing good deeds (Titus 2:14)

Questions:

1.) Do you feel you have benefited from the quality of being committed in your Christian walk? What is it about being committed represented in God's word that seems to really impact your life the most?

2.) What does scripture say about the quality of being committed for the believer (Deut. 30:20; Ps. 31:5; 2 Chron. 16:9; 17:6)?

3.) What is it about the quality of being committed that is important to living the providential life?

69. A believer has the quality of a **new life** when they come to know Christ as their Savior. The Christian has given up the life of this world and their new life is hidden with Christ (see Col. 3:3). This new life sets aim for the realities of heaven and where Christ will sit on His throne.

SCRIPTURAL PROVIDENTIAL INSIGHT

But now in Christ Jesus you who once were far off have been brought near by the blood of Christ. For he himself is our peace, who has made us both one and has broken down in his flesh the dividing wall of hostility by abolishing the law of commandments expressed in ordinances, that he might create in himself one new man in place of the two, so making peace, and might reconcile us both to God in one body through the cross, thereby killing the hostility. (Eph. 2:13–16 ESV)

Don't copy the behavior and customs of this world, but let God transform you into a new person by changing the way you think. Then you will learn to know God's will for you, which is good and pleasing and perfect. (Rom. 12:2)

Questions:

1.) Do you feel you have benefited from the quality of a new life in your Christian walk? What is it about the quality of a new life represented in God's word that seems to really impact your life the most?

2.) What does scripture say about the quality of a new life for the believer (Ezek. 36:26–27; Rom. 6:4; 2 Cor. 5:17; Gal. 6:15; Eph. 4:24; Col. 3:10; Heb. 10:20; Rev. 21:5)?

3.) What is it about the quality of a new life that is important to living the providential life?

70. A believer has **approval** as a saved child of God. The approval that a Christian receives is related to the goodness, peace and joy we receive in the Holy Spirit (see Rom. 14:17–18). Our approval is not related to anything we can do or earn but in what is provided to us through Jesus Christ and the Holy Spirit.

SCRIPTURAL PROVIDENTIAL INSIGHT

Therefore, I urge you, brothers and sisters, in view of God's mercy, to offer your bodies as a living sacrifice, holy and pleasing to God–this is your true and proper worship. Do not conform to the pattern of this world, but be transformed by the renewing of your mind. Then you will be able to test and approve what God's will is–his good, pleasing and perfect will. (Rom. 12:1–2 NIV)

For the kingdom of God is not a matter of what we eat or drink, but of living a life of goodness and peace and joy in the Holy Spirit. If you serve Christ with this attitude, you will please God, and others will approve of you, too. (Rom. 14:17–18)

Questions:

1.) Do you feel you have benefited from the quality of approval in your Christian walk? What is it about the quality of approval represented in God's word that seems to really impact your life the most?

2.) What does scripture say about the quality of approval for the believer (John 6:27; Rom. 2:18; 16:10; 1 Cor. 11:19; Gal. 1:10; 2 Tim. 2:15)?

3.) What is it about the quality of approval that is important to living the providential life?

11.7–MY STUDY GUIDE JOURNAL

Personal Reflections on My Study of a Providential Life

Called	**Reconciled**
Belong	**Blameless**
Adopted	**Committed**
Citizen	**New Life**
Chosen	**Approval**

71. A believer is **free** from sin through the knowledge of the truth (see John 8:32). The believer belongs to Jesus Christ and the life–giving Spirit frees us from sin and death (see Rom. 8:1–2). This freedom was possible because God sent His own Son in a body that satisfied the requirement of victory over sin.

Scriptural Providential Insight

Jesus replied, "I tell you the truth, everyone who sins is a slave of sin. A slave is not a permanent member of the family, but a son is part of the family forever. So if the Son sets you free, you are truly free." (John 8:34–36)

So now there is no condemnation for those who belong to Christ Jesus. And because you belong to him, the power of the life–giving Spirit has freed you from the power of sin that leads to death. (Rom. 8:1–2)

But when the right time came, God sent his Son, born of a woman, subject to the law. God sent him to buy freedom for us who were slaves to the law, so that he could adopt us as his very own children. (Gal. 4:4–5)

Questions:

1.) Do you feel you have benefited from the quality of being free in your Christian walk? What is it about the quality of being free represented in God's word that seems to really impact your life the most?

2.) What does scripture say about the quality of freedom for the believer (John 8:32; Rom. 3:24; 6:7; 6:18; Eph. 1:7; James 1:25; 1 Pet. 2:16)?

3.) What is it about the quality of being free that is important to living the providential life?

72. A believer's freedom is **bought** with the blood of Christ's sacrifice on the cross. Christ won this purchase for himself by his own blood. Our freedom as believers is therefore very precious and of inestimable value. Our freedom from sin and condemnation is not ours in any way; but, it was purchased by our Lord and Savior.

SCRIPTURAL PROVIDENTIAL INSIGHT

So guard yourselves and God's people. Feed and shepherd God's flock, his church, purchased with his own blood over which the Holy Spirit has appointed you as leaders. (Acts 20:28)

Don't you realize that your body is the temple of the Holy Spirit, who lives in you and was given to you by God? You do not belong to yourself, for God bought you with a high price. (1 Cor. 6:19–20a)

But there were also false prophets in Israel, just as there will be false teachers among you. They will cleverly teach destructive heresies and even deny the Master who bought them. In this way, they will bring sudden destruction on themselves. (2 Pet. 2:1)

Questions:

1.) Do you feel you have benefited from the quality of being bought in your Christian walk? What is it about the quality of being bought through the Savior's blood represented in God's word that seems to really impact your life the most?

2.) What does scripture say about the quality of being bought for the believer (1 Cor. 7:23; Eph. 1:7, 14; 1 Tim. 2:6; Col. 1:14; Heb. 9:7; 1 John 1:7; Rev. 1:5; 5:9; 14:4)?

3.) What is it about the quality of being bought through Christ's sacrifice that is important to living the providential life?

73. A believer in Jesus Christ is **filled with the Holy Spirit**. The Holy Spirit has been present since before creation and manifested its presence at the time of Pentecost (see Acts 2:4). The Spirit of God was poured out upon believers. Christ sent the Holy Spirit to earth to reside in believers, help the church spread throughout the world and further the plan of God.

SCRIPTURAL PROVIDENTIAL INSIGHT

And everyone present was filled with the Holy Spirit and began speaking in other languages, as the Holy Spirit gave them this ability. (Acts 2:4)

And this hope will not lead to disappointment. For we know how dearly God loves us, because he has given us the Holy Spirit to fill our hearts with his love. (Rom. 5:5)

Don't be drunk with wine, because that will ruin your life. Instead, be filled with the Holy Spirit, singing psalms and hymns and spiritual songs among yourselves, and making music to the Lord in your hearts. (Eph. 5:18–19)

Questions:

1.) Do you feel you have benefited from being filled with the Holy Spirit in your Christian walk? What is it about being filled with the Holy Spirit represented in God's word that seems to really impact your life the most?

2.) What does scripture say about the quality of being filled with the Holy Spirit for the believer (Luke 1:15, 41; 24:49; Acts 4:8–10, 31; 9:17–18; 13:9; Eph. 2:22; 1 Thess. 4:8)?

3.) What is it about the quality of being filled with the Holy Spirit that is important to living the providential life?

74. A believer should possess the quality of being **obedient** to Christ and the scriptures.

It is critical for the believer to not just hear the Word but obey. There is no reason to claim Christ as Lord and Savior unless one exhibits the obedience required as a believer. The Christian faith is not just of hearing but doing.

Scriptural Providential Insight

So why do you keep calling me "Lord, Lord!" when you don't do what I say? I will show you what it's like when someone comes to me, listens to my teaching and then follows it. (Luke 6:46–47)

Because one person disobeyed God, many became sinners. But because one other person obeyed God, many will be made righteous. (Rom. 5:19)

Even though Jesus was God's Son, he learned obedience from the things he suffered. (Heb. 5:8)

Questions:

1.) Do you feel you have benefited from obedience in your Christian walk? What is it about obedience represented in God's word that seems to really impact your life the most?

2.) What does scripture say about the quality obedience for the believer (Luke 11:28; 17:7–10; Mark 10:29–30; Rom. 16:26; Phil. 2:5–9; James 1:22–25; 1 Pet. 1:22; 1 John 3:18)?

3.) What is it about the quality of obedience that is important to living the providential life?

75. The Christian can rejoice when confronted with trials and problems for these are such a help in developing **endurance** in our faith. As a believer one suffers in various ways that reflect the life and values of Christ. A person of Christ then must bear these trials and maintains endurance to the end.

SCRIPTURAL PROVIDENTIAL INSIGHT

And all nations will hate you because you are my followers. But everyone who endures to the end will be saved. (Matt. 10:22)

We can rejoice, too, when we run into problems and trials, for we know that they help us develop endurance. And endurance develops strength of character, and character strengthens our confident hope of salvation. And this hope will not lead to disappointment. For we know how dearly God loves us, because he has given us the Holy Spirit to fill our hearts with his love. (Rom. 5:3–5)

God blesses those who patiently endure testing and temptation. Afterward they will receive the crown of life that God has promised to those who love him. (James 1:12)

Questions:

1.) Do you feel you have benefited from endurance in your Christian walk? What is it about endurance represented in God's word that seems to really impact your life the most?

2.) What does scripture say about the quality endurance for the believer (Mark 13:13; 2 Tim. 3:11; Heb. 10:36; 12:1–2; James 1:12; 5:11; Rev. 1:9)?

3.) What is it about the quality of endurance that is important to living the providential life?

76. The Christian inherits the characteristic of **courage** through the hope they have in their Lord and Savior Jesus Christ. When the disciples saw Jesus walking on the water in a horrible

storm they were terrified. Jesus reassured them and exhorted them to take courage because he was there with them (see Mark 6:49–50).

SCRIPTURAL PROVIDENTIAL INSIGHT

Be strong and courageous, for you are the one who will lead these people to possess all the land I swore to their ancestors I would give them. (Josh. 1:6)

But take courage! None of you will lose your lives, even though the ship will go down. For last night an angel of the God to whom I belong and whom I serve stood beside me, and he said, "Don't be afraid, Paul, for you will surely stand trial before Caesar! What's more, God in his goodness has granted safety to everyone sailing with you. So take courage!" For I believe God. (Acts 27:22–25)

But Christ, as the Son, is in charge of God's entire house. And we are God's house, if we keep our courage and remain confident in our hope in Christ. (Heb. 3:6)

Questions:

1.) Do you feel you have benefited from courage in your Christian walk? What is it about courage represented in God's word that seems to really impact your life the most?

2.) What does scripture say about the quality courage for the believer (Deut. 31:6; Judg. 5:21; Ps. 31:24; Mark 6:49–50; 1 Cor. 16:13–14; James 5:8; 1 John 2:28)?

3.) What is it about the quality of courage that is important to living the providential life?

77. The excitement that is generated by our Lord and Savior creates **enthusiasm** for the believer. Enthusiasm is an important quality for a Christian to have in influencing others in the cause of Christ. This was particularly true in the early church as the teachers and disciples spoke boldly in preaching the Gospel (see Acts 18:25).

SCRIPTURAL PROVIDENTIAL INSIGHT

He had been taught the way of the Lord, and he taught others about Jesus with an enthusiastic spirit and with accuracy. (Acts 18:25)

Dear brothers and sisters, the longing of my heart and my prayer to God is for the people of Israel to be saved. I know what enthusiasm they have for God, but it is misdirected zeal. For they don't understand God's way of making people right with himself. Refusing to accept God's way, they cling to their own way of getting right with God by trying to keep the law. (Rom. 10:1–3)

Work with enthusiasm, as though you were working for the Lord rather than for people. (Eph. 6:7)

Questions:

1.) Do you feel you have benefited from enthusiasm in your Christian walk? What is it about enthusiasm represented in God's word that seems to really impact your life the most?

2.) What does scripture say about the quality enthusiasm for the believer (Neh. 4:6; Ps. 45:15; Prov. 19:2; 2 Cor. 8:7,16; 9:2)?

3.) What is it about the quality of enthusiasm that is important to living the providential life?

78. The believer has the perfect **example** to follow in that of Jesus Christ. Christ desired his disciples exemplify the actions that He had done while on earth (see John 13:15). The Old Testament holds many examples of key figures that embody characteristic strengths and qualities of Christ. Christ represents the final prophet, king and priest that fulfills the prophecies and functions of these character types.

SCRIPTURAL PROVIDENTIAL INSIGHT

I have given you an example to follow. Do as I have done to you. I tell you the truth, slaves are not greater than their master. Nor is the messenger more important than the one who sends the message. Now that you know these things, God will bless you for doing them. (John 13:15–17)

And you yourself must be an example to them by doing good works of every kind. Let everything you do reflect the integrity and seriousness of your teaching. Teach the truth so that your teaching can't be criticized. Then those who oppose us will be ashamed and have nothing bad to say about us. (Titus 2:7–8)

Questions:

1.) Do you feel you have benefited from being an example in your Christian walk? What is it about being an example represented in God's word that seems to really impact your life the most?

2.) What does scripture say about the quality of example for the believer (Phil. 3:17; 1 Thess. 1:7; 2 Thess. 3:7; 1 Tim. 4:12; Heb. 13:7; James 5:10)?

3.) What is it about the quality of example that is important to living the providential life?

79. God pronounced the creation as **good** in the book of Genesis. God is referred to as good in many places throughout Scripture (see 2 Chron. 7:3). According to Jesus, only God is truly good (see Mark 10:18). Jesus refers to examples in the parables in many places in the Gospels as good to illustrate an example of goodness.

SCRIPTURAL PROVIDENTIAL INSIGHT

The master was full of praise. "Well done, my good and faithful servant. (Matt. 25:21)

A good person produces good things from the treasury of a good heart, and an evil person produces evil things from the treasury of an evil heart. (Luke 6:45)

And I know that nothing good lives in me, that is, in my sinful nature. I want to do what is right, but I can't. I want to do what is good but I don't. I don't want to do what is wrong, but I do it anyway. (Rom. 7:18–19)

Questions:

1.) Do you feel you have benefited from being good in your Christian walk? What is it about being good represented in God's word that seems to really impact your life the most?

2.) What does scripture say about the quality of being good for the believer (Gen. 1:4; 2 Chron. 31:20; Ps. 34:8; Isa. 5:20; Matt. 22:10; Mark 3:4; Luke 18:19; Rom. 12:9; James 2:8)?

3.) What is it about the quality of being good that is important to living the providential life?

80. The believer is **glad** to receive the message of the Gospel. A Christian is naturally glad for the forgiveness of sins and the promise of eternity that they enjoy. Even when suffering persecution the believer should be glad for the reward that awaits in heaven. All who are chosen to become believers are glad.

Scriptural Providential Insight

No wonder my heart is glad, and I rejoice. My body rests in safety. For you will not leave my soul among the dead or allow your holy one to rot in the grave. You will show me the way of life, granting me the joy of your presence and the pleasures of living with you forever. (Ps. 16:9–11)

Be happy about it! Be very glad! For a great reward awaits you in heaven. And remember, the ancient prophets were persecuted in the same way. (Matt. 5:12)

Let us be glad and rejoice, and let us give honor to him. For the time has come for the wedding feast of the Lamb, and his bride has prepared herself. (Rev. 19:7)

Questions:

1.) Do you feel you have benefited from being glad in your Christian walk? What is it about being glad represented in God's word that seems to really impact your life the most?

2.) What does scripture say about the quality of being glad for the believer (Ps. 32:11, 69:32; 118:24; Prov. 10:8; 27:11; Isa. 35:1; Zeph. 3:14; Acts 13:48; 1 Cor. 12:26)?

3.) What is it about the quality of being glad that is important to living the providential life?

11.8–MY STUDY GUIDE JOURNAL

Personal Reflections on My Study of a Providential Life

Free	**Courage**
Bought	**Enthusiasm**
Filled with the Holy Spirit	**Examples**
Obedient	**Good**
Endurance	**Glad**

81. The believer experiences **victory** through Christ over sin, death and hell. Christ fulfilled the prophecy predicting justice to be victorious (see Matt. 12:20). Eternal blessing and rewards are to be the result of those that are victorious in their faith in Jesus Christ (see Rev. 2:26). The word for "victory" is included over sixty times in scripture.

SCRIPTURAL PROVIDENTIAL INSIGHTS

How the king rejoices in your strength, O Lord! He shouts with joy because you give him victory. (Ps. 21:1)

The Lord has demonstrated his holy power before the eyes of all the nations. All the ends of the earth will see the victory of our God. (Isa. 52:10)

All who are victorious will inherit all these blessings, and I will be their God, and they will be my children. (Rev. 21:7)

Questions:

1.) Do you feel you have benefited from being victorious in your Christian walk? What is it about victory represented in God's word that seems to really impact your life the most?

2.) What does scripture say about the quality of victory for the believer (2 Sam. 8:6; Isa. 53:12; Matt. 12:20; Rom. 8:37; 1 Cor. 15:54; Col. 2:15; Rev. 2:11,17, 26; 3:5, 21; 21:7)?

3.) What is it about the quality of victory that is important to living the providential life?

82. The believer is **saved** from sin, death and hell through their Lord and Savior Jesus Christ. Scripture indicates the saving power of the Lord (see Ps. 68:20). The purpose of Christ's ministry is rooted in His saving power (see John 12:47). The destiny of mankind is death that can only be averted by the saving that comes with the forgiveness of our sins (see James 5:20).

SCRIPTURAL PROVIDENTIAL INSIGHT

Our God is a God who saves! The Sovereign Lord rescues us from death. (Ps. 68:20)

And she will have a son, and you are to name him Jesus, for he will save his people from their sins. (Matt. 1:21)

It is this Good News that saves you if you continue to believe the message I told you unless, of course, you believed something that was never true in the first place. (1 Cor. 15:2)

Questions:

1.) How do you feel you have benefited from being saved in your Christian walk? What is it about being saved represented in God's word that seems to really impact your life the most?

2.) What does scripture say about the quality of being saved for the believer (Matt. 24:13; John 10:9; 12:47; Acts 4:12; 16:30; Rom. 1:6; 5:9; 10:9; 1 Cor. 1:18; 10:33; Eph. 1:13; 1 Thess. 5:9; 1 Tim. 1:15; 5:9; 2 Tim. 1:9; Titus 3:5; Heb. 7:25; James 5:20; 2 Pet. 3:15)?

3.) What is it about the quality of being saved that is important to living the providential life?

83. The believer is **renewed** through the saving action of our Lord and Savior Jesus Christ that removes sin. The experience of being born again leads naturally to a renewed experience in the life of a Christian (see Eph. 4:23). The Holy Spirit gives the believer a renewal of the mind and spirit that has a purifying effect upon the soul.

SCRIPTURAL PROVIDENTIAL INSIGHT

Create in me a clean heart, O God, and renew a right spirit within me. (Ps. 51:10 ESV)

Even youths shall faint and be weary, and young men shall fall exhausted; but they who wait for the Lord shall renew their strength; they shall mount up with wings like eagles; they shall run and not be weary; they shall walk and not faint. (Isa. 40:30–31 ESV)

Jesus said to them, "Truly I tell you, at the renewal of all things, when the Son of Man is seated on the throne of his glory, you who have followed me will also sit on twelve thrones, judging the twelve tribes of Israel." (Matt. 19:28 NRSV)

Questions:

1.) Do you feel you have benefited from being renewed in your Christian walk? What is it about being renewed represented in God's word that seems to really impact your life the most?

2.) What does scripture say about the quality of renewal for the believer (Ps. 103:5; 2 Cor. 4:16; Eph. 4:23; Col. 3:10)?

3.) What is it about the quality of renewal that is important to living the providential life?

84. The believer is **transformed** through the power of God. A believer is fundamentally changed in their thinking and reasoning. Wisdom is imparted to the Christian from God through the Holy Spirit and Jesus Christ. Our entire mental status is radically changed as a result of our conversion process.

SCRIPTURAL PROVIDENTIAL INSIGHT

Don't copy the behavior and customs of this world, but let God transform you into a new person by changing the way you think. Then you will learn to know God's will for you, which is good and pleasing and perfect. (Rom. 12:2)

And we all, with unveiled face, beholding the glory of the Lord, are being transformed into the same image from one degree of glory to another. For this comes from the Lord who is the Spirit. (2 Cor. 3:18 ESV)

But our citizenship is in heaven, and from it we await a Savior, the Lord Jesus Christ, who will transform our lowly body to be like his glorious body, by the power that enables him even to subject all things to himself. (Phil. 3:20–21 ESV)

Questions:

1.) Do you feel you have benefited from being transformed in your Christian walk? What is it about being transformed represented in God's word that seems to really impact your life the most?

2.) What does Scripture say about the quality of being transformed for the believer (Rom. 12:2; 1 Cor. 15:51; 2 Cor. 3:18; Phil. 3:21)?

3.) What is it about the quality of being transformed that is important to living the providential life?

85. The believer is united with Christ in the **death** of our old sinful selves. The Christian believer dies to the sin that Adam brought into the world and spread to everyone (see Rom. 5:12). Christ brought new life into the world through his act of righteousness that brings a correct relationship and reconciliation to God (see Rom. 5:18).

SCRIPTURAL PROVIDENTIAL INSIGHT

When Adam sinned, sin entered the world. Adam's sin brought death, so death spread to everyone, for everyone sinned. (Rom. 5:12)

Yes, Adam's one sin brings condemnation for everyone, but Christ's one act of righteousness brings a right relationship with God and new life for everyone. Because one person disobeyed God, many became sinners. But because one other person obeyed God, many will be made righteous. (Rom. 5:18–19)

But let me reveal to you a wonderful secret. We will not all die, but we will all be transformed! (1 Cor. 15:51)

Questions:

1.) Do you feel you have benefited from your death to sin in your Christian walk? What is it about being dead to sin represented in God's word that seems to really impact your life the most?

2.) What does scripture say about the quality of death to sin for the believer (Isa. 38:17; Rom. 6:23; 7:24; 1 Cor. 15:26; 2 Cor. 3:6; Gal. 3:1; 2 Tim. 1:10; Heb. 2:14; 1 Pet. 2:24)?

3.) What is it about the quality of being dead to sin that is important to living the providential life?

86. The believer is made **clean** in their relationship with God through the sacrifice of Christ on the cross. We are to be pure in our living so that we can be clean in our use by God in every good work (see 2 Tim. 2:21). The Spirit of God has made us holy and the blood of Jesus Christ has cleansed us (see 1 Peter 1:2).

SCRIPTURAL PROVIDENTIAL INSIGHT

How can I know all the sins lurking in my heart? Cleanse me from these hidden faults. Keep your servant from deliberate sins! Don't let them control me. Then I will be free of guilt and innocent of great sin. (Ps. 19:12–13)

Some of you were once like that. But you were cleansed; you were made holy; you were made right with God by calling on the name of the Lord Jesus Christ and by the Spirit of our God. (1 Cor. 6:11)

God the Father knew you and chose you long ago, and his Spirit has made you holy. As a result, you have obeyed him and have been cleansed by the blood of Christ. (1 Pet. 1:2)

Questions:

1.) Do you feel you have benefited from being made clean in your Christian walk? What is it about being made clean represented in God's word that seems to really impact your life the most?

2.) What does scripture say about the quality of being made clean for the believer (Ps. 51:2,7,10; Acts 15:9; 2 Cor. 7:1; 2 Tim. 2:21; Titus 2:14; Heb. 1:3; 1 Pet. 1:22; 1 John 1:9)?

3.) What is it about the quality of being made clean that is important to living the providential life?

87. The believer is made **complete** with all other believers in order to show the unity of the body of Christ. A Christian is made complete when their faith and their actions work together (see James 2:22). The standard for the believer is the unity and faith that makes us complete as an example of the standards of Christ (see Eph. 4:11–13). The New Testament mentions the word complete some seventy-six times in the NRSV translation.

SCRIPTURAL PROVIDENTIAL INSIGHT

For he will complete what he appoints for me, and many such things are in his mind. (Job 23:14 ESV)

This will continue until we all come to such unity in our faith and knowledge of God's Son that we will be mature in the Lord, measuring up to the full and complete standard of Christ. (Eph. 4:13)

For you know that when your faith is tested, your endurance has a chance to grow. So let it grow, for when your endurance is fully developed, you will be perfect and complete, needing nothing. (James 1:3–4)

Questions:

1.) Do you feel you have benefited from being made complete in your Christian walk? What is it about being made complete as represented in God's word that seems to really impact your life the most?

2.) What does scripture say about the quality of being complete for the believer (John 15:11; 16:24; Rom. 15:28; 1 Cor. 13:10; 2 Cor. 8:6; Phil. 2:2; James 1:4; 2:22; 2 John 12)?

3.) What is it about the quality of being made complete that is important to living the providential life?

88. The believer is **devoted** to God. The Christian life requires a singular devotion to God (see Matt. 6:24). A Christian should show devotion by living in faith, love, holiness and modesty (see 1 Tim. 4:15). Devotion is a quality that demands many other qualities to be considered a person that defines it.

SCRIPTURAL PROVIDENTIAL INSIGHT

No one can serve two masters. For you will hate one and love the other; you will be devoted to one and despise the other. You cannot serve God and be enslaved to money. (Matt. 6:24)

You know that Stephanas and his household were the first of the harvest of believers in Greece, and they are spending their lives in service to God's people. I urge you, dear brothers and sisters, to submit to them and others like them who serve with such devotion. (1 Cor. 16:15–16)

Rather, he must enjoy having guests in his home, and he must love what is good. He must live wisely and be just. He must live a devout and disciplined life. (Titus 1:8)

Questions:

1.) Do you feel you have benefited from being devout in your Christian walk? What is it about being devoted as represented in God's word that seems to really impact your life the most?

2.) What does scripture say about the quality of being a devoted believer (2 Chron. 32:32; Ps. 86:2; Acts 10:2; Col. 2:23; 2 Cor. 11:3; 1 Tim. 5:11; Titus 1:8)?

3.) What is it about the quality of devotion that is important in living the providential life?

89. A believer **grows** in their grace and faith in Jesus Christ as they mature. The growth of a believer is ultimately dependent only upon God (see 1 Cor. 3:5–7). As we mature we will speak the truth in love, growing in every way to be more like Christ (see Eph. 4:15). The growth of a Christian allows joy in our faith (see Phil. 1:25).

SCRIPTURAL PROVIDENTIAL INSIGHT

I planted the seed in your hearts, and Apollos watered it, but it was God who made it grow. It's not important who does the planting, or who does the watering. What's important is that God makes the seed grow. (1 Cor. 3:6)

He makes the whole body fit together perfectly. As each part does its own special work, it helps the other parts grow, so that the whole body is healthy and growing and full of love. (Eph. 4:16)

Rather, you must grow in the grace and knowledge of our Lord and Savior Jesus Christ. All glory to him, both now and forever! Amen. (2 Pet. 3:18)

Questions:

1.) Do you feel you have benefited from growth in your Christian walk? What is it about growth as represented in God's word that seems to really impact your life the most?

2.) What does scripture say about the quality of growth for the believer (1 Cor. 3:6; Eph. 4:16; Phil. 1:25; Col. 2:19; 2 Thess. 1:3; James 1:15; 2 Pet. 3:18)?

3.) What is it about the quality of growth that is important to living the providential life?

90. A believer has come to **know** that Jesus Christ is their Lord and Savior and the Holy One of God. The believer acknowledges a God that knows when the slightest thing happens in His creation (see Matt. 10:29). The Christian has no doubt about who is the Savior of the world. We know this is true (see John 4:42).

Scriptural Providential Insight

I will claim you as my own people, and I will be your God. Then you will know that I am the Lord your God who has freed you from your oppression in Egypt. (Exod. 6:7)

I have given you an example to follow. Do as I have done to you. I tell you the truth, slaves are not greater than their master. Nor is the messenger more important than the one who sends the message. Now that you know these things, God will bless you for doing them. (John 13:15–17)

That is why I am suffering here in prison. But I am not ashamed of it, for I know the one in whom I trust, and I am sure that he is able to guard what I have entrusted to him until the day of his return. (2 Tim. 1:12)

Questions:

1.) Do you feel you have benefited from knowing in your Christian walk? What is it about knowing as represented in God's word that seems to really impact your life the most?

2.) What does scripture say about the quality of knowing for the believer (Gen. 3:5; Exod. 6:7; Deut. 18:21; Job 19:25; Ps. 94:11; Jer. 31:34; Dan. 11:32; John 2:24–25; 1 John 2:3; Rev. 3:15)?

3.) What is it about the quality of know that is important to living the providential life?

11.9–MY STUDY GUIDE JOURNAL

Personal Reflections on My Study of a Providential Life

Victorious	**Clean**
Saved	**Complete**
Renewed	**Devotion**
Transformed	**Grows**
Died with Christ	**Know**

91. God inspires **confidence** in the believer (see Phil. 2:24). The boldness of Christians in proclaiming the Gospel inspires confidence in other believers (see Phil. 1:14). The believer has confidence in the mercy and grace that follows them in their time of need (see Heb. 4:16).

SCRIPTURAL PROVIDENTIAL INSIGHT

This is what the Sovereign Lord, the Holy One of Israel, says: "Only in returning to me and resting in me will you be saved. In quietness and confidence is your strength. But you would have none of it." (Isa. 30:15)

And because of my imprisonment, most of the believers here have gained confidence and boldly speak God's message without fear. (Phil. 1:14)

Because of that experience, we have even greater confidence in the message proclaimed by the prophets. You must pay close attention to what they wrote, for their words are like a lamp shining in a dark place until the Day dawns, and Christ the Morning Star shines in your hearts. (2 Pet. 1:19)

Questions:

1.) Do you feel you have benefited from confidence in your Christian walk? What is it about confidence as represented in God's word that seems to really impact your life the most?

2.) What does scripture say about the quality of confidence for the believer (Ps. 146:3; 2 Cor. 8:22; Phil. 2:24; 3:4; Col. 2:2; 1 Thess. 5:8; Titus 1:2; 1 John 4:17)?

3.) What is it about the quality of confidence that is important to living the providential life?

92. A Christian's endurance through various trials increases the **character** of the person (see Rom. 5:4). Endurance through the process of suffering results in character that is refined and purified. We can be corrupted through the bad company of those we associate (see 1 Cor. 15:33).

SCRIPTURAL PROVIDENTIAL INSIGHT

We can rejoice, too, when we run into problems and trials, for we know that they help us develop endurance. And endurance develops strength of character, and character strengthens our confident hope of salvation. (Rom. 5:3–4)

Don't be fooled by those who say such things, for "bad company corrupts good character." (1 Cor. 15:33)

The Son radiates God's own glory and expresses the very character of God, and he sustains everything by the mighty power of his command. When he had cleansed us from our sins, he sat down in the place of the right hand of the majestic God in heaven. (Heb. 1:3)

Questions:

1.) Do you feel you have benefited from character in your Christian walk? What is it about character as represented in God's word that seems to really impact your life the most?

2.) What does scripture say about the quality of character for the believer (Rom. 5:4; 1 Cor. 15:33; 2 Cor. 12:7; Heb. 1:3)?

3.) What is it about the quality of character that is important to living the providential life?

93. The Christian finds that with God all things are **possible**. The concept of the word possible takes on a whole new meaning for the believer (see Matt. 19:26; Mark 10:27; Luke 18:27). Belief is a key component in the Christian concept of anything being possible (see Mark 9:23).

SCRIPTURAL PROVIDENTIAL INSIGHT

Jesus looked at them intently and said, "Humanly speaking, it is impossible. But with God everything is possible." (Matt. 19:26)

What do you mean, 'If I can'? "Jesus asked. "Anything is possible if a person believes." (Mark 9:23)

For it is not possible for the blood of bulls and goats to take away sins. That is why, when Christ came into the world, he said to God, "You did not want animal sacrifices or sin offerings. But you have given me a body to offer." (Heb. 10:4-5)

Questions:

1.) Do you feel you have benefited from all things are possible in your Christian walk? What is it about all things are possible as represented in God's word that seems to really impact your life the most?

2.) What does scripture say about the quality of all things are possible for the believer (Matt. 19:26; 26:39; Mark 9:23; 10:27; 14:35; Luke 18:27; Heb. 10:4)?

3.) What is it about the quality of all things are possible that is important to living the providential life?

94. The way of the Lord is **prepared.** The way prepared for the Lord will be seen by all of the people together (see Isa. 40:3). God has prepared the way of the Lord through the salvation made possible through Jesus Christ to inherit the kingdom of God.

Scriptural Providential Insight

Then the King will say to those on his right, 'Come you who are blessed by my Father, inherit the kingdom prepared for you from the creation of the world.' (Matt. 25:34)

Don't let your hearts be troubled. Trust in God, and trust also in me. There is more than enough room in my Father's home. If this were not so, would I have told you that I am going to prepare a place for you? When everything is ready, I will come and get you, so that you will always be with me where I am. (John 14:1–3)

God himself has prepared us for this, and as a guarantee he has given us his Holy Spirit. (2 Cor. 5:5)

Questions:

1.) Do you feel you have benefited from being prepared in your Christian walk? What is it about being prepared as represented in God's word that seems to really impact your life the most?

2.) What does scripture say about the quality of being prepared for the believer (Exod. 23:20; Ps. 23:5; Zeph. 1:7; Mal. 3:1; Matt. 3:3; 1 Cor. 2:9; 2 Tim. 4:2; 1 Pet. 1:13)?

3.) What is it about the quality of being prepared that is important to living the providential life?

95. Christ as a **holy** sacrifice made possible the holiness of believers as holy through the truth of God (see John 17:17). The believer is called upon to live a life that is holy (see 1 Thess. 4:7). God's salvation and our being made holy are all part of the plan He has had since the beginning of time (see 2 Tim. 1:9).

SCRIPTURAL PROVIDENTIAL INSIGHT

Make them holy by your truth; teach them your word, which is truth. Just as you sent me into the world, I am sending them into the world. And I give myself as a holy sacrifice for them so they can be made holy by your truth. (John 17:17–19)

I am a special messenger from Christ Jesus to you Gentiles. I bring you the Good News so that I might present you as an acceptable offering to God, made holy by the Holy Spirit. (Rom. 15:16)

God has called us to live holy lives, not impure lives. Therefore, anyone who refuses to live by these rules is not disobeying human teaching but is rejecting God, who gives his Holy Spirit to you. (1 Thess. 4:7–8)

Questions:

1.) Do you feel you have benefited from being holy in your Christian walk? What is it about being holy as represented in God's word that seems to really impact your life the most?

2.) What does scripture say about the quality of being holy for the believer (Ps. 22:3; Isa. 54:5; Mark 1:24; Luke 1:35; John 17:17; Rom. 7:12; 1 Cor. 1:30; Eph. 4:24; Col. 1:22; 1 Thess. 5:23; 1 Tim. 1:9; Heb. 10:13–14; 13:12; 1 Pet. 1:16; 2 Pet. 2:21; Rev. 3:7)?

3.) What is it about the quality of being holy that is important to living the providential life?

96. Through the coming of Jesus Christ and His sacrifice on the cross the **value** of the believer grew. Christ made it clear to the people He spoke to that they were valuable to God (see Matt. 10:28–31; Luke 12:23–24). You were so important to God that He gave his only Son so that you would not perish and have eternal life (see John 3:16).

SCRIPTURAL PROVIDENTIAL INSIGHT

So don't be afraid; you are more valuable to God than a whole flock of sparrows. (Matt. 10:31)

Again, the kingdom of heaven is like a merchant on the lookout for choice pearls. When he discovered a pearl of great value, he sold everything he owned and bought it! (Matt. 13:45–46)

But on judgment day, fire will reveal what kind of work each builder has done. The fire will show if a person's work has any value. (1 Cor. 3:13)

Questions:

1.) Do you feel you have benefited from having value in your Christian walk? What is it about value as represented in God's word that seems to really impact your life the most?

2.) What does scripture say about the quality of value for the believer (Job 28:17; Ps. 119:72; Luke 12:24; Phil. 3:7–8)?

3.) What is it about the quality of God's perceived value of you that is important to living the providential life?

97. God is **able** to accomplish in the believer more than we might ask or think (see Eph. 3:20). No power is able to separate us from the love of God that is revealed in Christ our Lord (see Rom. 8:39). The Holy Spirit caused believers to be able to function in all new ways at Pentecost (see Acts 2:1–6).

SCRIPTURAL PROVIDENTIAL INSIGHT

And everyone present was filled with the Holy Spirit and began speaking in other languages, as the Holy Spirit gave them this ability. (Acts 2:4)

A servant of the Lord must not quarrel but must be kind to everyone, be able to teach, and be patient with difficult people. (2 Tim. 2:24)

We think you ought to know, dear brothers and sisters, about the trouble we went through in the province of Asia. We were crushed and overwhelmed beyond our ability to endure, and we thought we would never live through it. In fact, we expected to die. But as a result, we stopped relying on ourselves and learned to rely only on God, who raises the dead. (2 Cor. 1:8–9)

Questions:

1.) Do you feel you have benefited from being able in your Christian walk? What is it about being able as represented in God's word that seems to really impact your life the most?

2.) What does scripture say about the quality of being able for the believer (Exod. 35:34; Deut. 16:17; Dan. 3:17; Rom. 8:39; Eph. 3:20; 2 Tim. 1:12; Jude 24)?

3.) What is it about the quality of being able that is important to living the providential life?

98. The Bible warns the believer to be **alert** to future events such as conquering invaders and the return of Jesus Christ (see Mark 13:33). The Christian is warned to be alert for their great enemy, the devil (see 1 Pet. 5:8). Believers are to be alert and pray in the Spirit at all times (see Eph. 6:18).

Scriptural Providential Insight

However, no one knows the day or hour when these things will happen, not even the angels in heaven or the Son himself. Only the Father knows. And since you don't know when that time will come, be on guard! Stay alert! (Mark 13:32–33)

In all circumstances take up the shield of faith, with which you can extinguish all the flaming darts of the evil one; and take the helmet of salvation, and the sword of the Spirit, which is the word of God, praying at all times in the Spirit, with all prayer and supplication. To that end keep alert with all perseverance, making supplication for all the saints, and also for me, that words may be given to me in opening my mouth boldly to proclaim the mystery of the gospel, for which I am ambassador in chains, that I may declare it boldly, as I ought to speak. (Eph. 6:16–20 ESV)

Questions:

1.) Do you feel you have benefited from being alert in your Christian walk? What is it about being alert as represented in God's word that seems to really impact your life the most?

2.) What does scripture say about the quality of being alert for the believer (Isa. 21:7; Mark 13:33; Acts 20:31; Eph. 6:18; 1 Pet. 5:8)?

3.) What is it about the quality of being alert that is important to living the providential life?

99. Believers that become like little **children** will enter the kingdom in heaven (see Matt. 18:2–4; Mark 10:15). Those that are in Christ will through faith become children of God (see Gal. 3:26). Christ said that those who work for peace will be called the children of God (see Matt. 5:9).

SCRIPTURAL PROVIDENTIAL INSIGHT

Then he said, "I tell you the truth, unless you turn from your sins and become like little children, you will never get into the kingdom of heaven. (Matt. 18:3)

Then Jesus called for the children and said to the disciples, "Let the children come to me. Don't stop them! For the kingdom of God belongs to those to those who are like these children. I tell you the truth, anyone who doesn't receive the kingdom of God like a child will never enter it." (Luke 18:16–17)

For you are all children of God through faith in Christ Jesus. (Gal. 3:26)

Questions:

1.) Do you feel you have benefited from being a child of God in your Christian walk? What is it about being a child of God as represented in God's word that seems to really impact your life the most?

2.) What does scripture say about the quality of being a child of God for the believer (Matt. 5:9; Mark 10:15; Luke 6:35; John 1:12; Rom. 9:26; Gal. 3:26; Eph. 3:6; Heb. 12:7)?

3.) What is it about the quality of being a child of God that is important to living the providential life?

100. The believer in Jesus Christ purifies our sinful deeds so that we can **worship** the living God (see Heb. 9:14). True worshippers of the Father must worship Him in spirit and in truth (see John 4:24). When a believer presents their body as a living sacrifice to God this is considered their spiritual worship (see Rom. 12:1).

SCRIPTURAL PROVIDENTIAL INSIGHT

For God is Spirit, so those who worship him must worship in spirit and truth. (John 4:24)

Just think how much more the blood of Christ will purify our consciences from sinful deeds so that we can worship the living God. For by the power of the eternal Spirit, Christ offered himself to God as a perfect sacrifice for our sins. (Heb. 9:14)

I appeal to you therefore, brothers, by the mercies of God, to present your bodies as a living sacrifice, holy and acceptable to God, which is your spiritual worship. (Rom. 12:1 ESV)

Questions:

1.) Do you feel you have benefited from worship of God in your Christian walk? What is it about worship of God as represented in God's word that seems to really impact your life the most?

2.) What does scripture say about the quality of worship of God for the believer (Gen. 12:8; 2 Kings 17:36; Ps. 29:2; Luke 23:47; John 4:24; Heb. 9:14)?

3.) What is it about the quality of worship of God that is important to living the providential life?

11.10–My Study Guide Journal

Personal Reflections on My Study of a Providential Life

Confidence	**Value**
Character	**Able**
Possible	**Alert**
Prepared	**Children**
Holy	**Worship**

CHAPTER TWELVE

Reflections on the Nature of God's Providence and Providential Living

There are several observations that we need to reflect upon before we begin to engage in Providential Living. These observations will enable us to approach living for God in a scriptural manner while acknowledging limitations and pitfalls that can plague a believer.

1. Only God can comprehend the full extent of His providence. This needs to be a remembered concept as we seek to pursue the act of living providentially. "The Lord our God has secrets known to no one. We are not accountable for them, but we and our children are accountable forever for all that he has revealed to us, so that we may obey all the terms of these instructions" (Deut. 29:29). Here we are reminded that we are only accountable for the revelation that God has provided to us. We need to remain in an attitude of trust and humility when we consider the will of God in our lives.

2. The providence of God is planned before all human events and extends to eternity. "You saw me before I was born. Every day of my life was recorded in your book. Every moment was laid out before a single day had passed. How precious are your thoughts about me, O God. They cannot be numbered! I can't even count them; they outnumber the grains of sand! And when I wake up, you are still with me" (Ps. 139:16–18)!

3. God will lead us upon the venture we are on to eternal life if we trust Him in our lives. "Search me, O God, and know my heart; trust me and know my anxious thoughts. Point out anything in me that offends you, and lead me along the path of everlasting life" (Ps. 139:23–24).

4. God created the heavens and earth as a place to be lived in by His creation. "For the Lord is God, and he created the heavens and earth and put everything in place. He made the world to be lived in, not to be a place of empty chaos. 'I am the Lord,' he says, 'and there is no other'"

(Isa. 45:18). A high purpose of the providence of God is to call out those who will acknowledge Him as their God. "Bring all who claim me as their God, for I have made them for my glory. It was I who created them" (Isa. 43:7).

5. God has revealed His perfect instructions, decrees, commandments and laws to the believer. "The instructions of the Lord are perfect, reviving the soul. The decrees of the Lord are trustworthy, making wise the simple. The commandments of the Lord are right, bringing joy to the heart. The commands of the Lord are clear, giving insight for living. Reverence for the Lord is pure, lasting forever. The laws of the Lord are true; each one is fair" (Ps. 19:7–9).

6. God has brought us the Good News through Jesus Christ and in so doing insured that he never left us without evidence of Himself and His goodness. Paul and Barnabas bring this point home in Acts. "We are merely human beings, just like you! We have come to bring you the Good News that you should turn from these worthless things and turn to the living God, who made heaven and earth, the sea, and everything in them. In the past he permitted all the nations to go their own ways, but he never left them without evidence of himself and his goodness" (Acts 14:15–17).

7. God's will is for the believer to obtain an inheritance which is according to His will and is guaranteed by the Holy Spirit. "In him we have obtained an inheritance, having been predestined according to the purpose of him who works all things according to the counsel of his will, so that we who were the first to hope in Christ might be to the praise of his glory. In him you also, when you heard the word of truth, the gospel of your salvation, and believed in him were sealed with the promised Holy Spirit, who is the guarantee of our inheritance until we acquire possession of it, to the praise of his glory" (Eph. 1:11–14 ESV).

8. God has worked his will through Christ to create all things, hold all creation together, and reconcile everything to himself (see Col. 1:16–20).

9. When the believer arrives in heaven it will be the will of God for Him to receive glory, honor and power. "You are worthy, O Lord our God, to receive glory and honor and power. For you created all things, and they exist because you created what you pleased" (Rev. 4:11). Christ will also be worshiped by innumerable beings and angels in heaven (see Rev. 5:11–14).

10. One needs to be cautious in the interpretation on an individual life or the world stage of how the providence of God is manifesting itself. We have only limited abilities to interpret the providence of God. God's infinitely complex weave of His providential will is far beyond our capabilities to comprehend and must severely limit our human ability to interpret or know.

Chapter Thirteen

Pursuing Providential Living in Your Life

This study guide and journal can be (but is not limited to being) a follow-up on the original book, *Living A Providential Life: Discovering Providential Qualities to Live By,* and give readers an opportunity to explore in a personal way the key points and qualities discussed in that book. This exploration has used the following methods:

1. An expanded use of scripture references of the individual qualities have been utilized to study in-depth meaning attached to each.

2. An attempt to discover personal benefits attached to each quality was explored through questioning involving each quality.

3. The importance of each quality, as it is linked to the overall goal of the book *Living the Providential Life,* was investigated.

4. A personal "My Study Guide Journal" was provided in the many appropriate segments of this book to record personal reflections on the study of a providential life.

5. The study in this book is designed to be another stepping stone to an enriching pursuit of providential life that is personally discovered and applied to each reader's exploration of the subject.

The subject of providence is inexhaustible and affords the interested person a wealth of opportunities for further exploration on the subject. This subject is exciting, rewarding and practical to study and apply in our lives. What can be more worthwhile than studying the will of God in our world and our lives? It makes enormous sense to synchronize the purpose and will of our lives to that of our God. The inevitable result is victory and success through Jesus Christ our Savior. We can rely on our powerful, righteous and forgiving Lord as we seek to live our lives in coordination with His providential purpose and plan.

If you make the Lord your refuge, if you make the Most High your shelter, no evil will conquer you; no plague will come near your home. For he will order his angels to protect you wherever you go. They will hold you up with their hands so you won't even hurt your foot on a stone. You will trample upon lions and cobras; you will crush fierce lions and serpents under your feet! The Lord says, "I will rescue those who love me. I will protect those who trust in my name. When they call on me, I will answer; I will be with them in trouble. I will rescue and honor them. I will reward them with a long life and give them my salvation." (Ps. 91:9–16)

Let us seek to "live in the shelter of the Most High" where we "will find rest in the shadow of the Almighty" (Ps. 91:1). We strive to be Christians and exemplify the qualities that scripture calls for in a believer. These qualities represent wise instruction for the believer in their search for obedience and love of Jesus Christ. "Keep hold of instruction; do not let go; guard her, for she is your life" (Prov. 4:13 ESV).

God reaches out to us in the revelation of scripture to guide us in His will. God also uses every experience in your life, good and bad, to work for the goodness of His will. "And we know that God causes everything to work together for the good of those who love God and are called according to his purpose for them" (Rom. 8:28). God controls everything in our lives to work for our good as people who love Him.

The pursuit of providential living is different for every person. Every aspect of a person's life is pertinent to this pursuit and; therefore, every part of your life is important in living as God desires. Your occupation, relaxation, family, friends, vacations, weekends, entertainment, Bible study and worship time are all key parts in providential living. Your life and the effort you make in coordinating it with God's providential plan will depend upon a large number of factors. One of those is how you absorb and exemplify the providential qualities that Jesus possessed and emulate these in your life. The character of Jesus should be the standard that we try to aspire to as a Christian.

We can be assured that God's plan can accommodate the good and bad decisions that we make every day. At the same time, God's providential plan is powerful beyond our ability to comprehend it. This power cannot be thwarted by anything we as an individual or group of individuals may try to change. God has an infinite number of methods to guide us into tracks that will comply with His will and plan. We can live in ways we think are independent of external influence; however, ultimately these pathways are either with or against God's will and in the end God's will is achieved.

Scripture tells us to imitate God and follow the example of Christ. "Imitate God, in everything you do, because you are his dear children. Live a life filled with love, following the example of Christ" (Eph. 5:1–2). We need to imitate and follow the example of our God and Christ.

"Carefully determine what pleases the Lord" (Eph. 5:10). It follows that studying the qualities of our Father God and Jesus Christ can help us follow the example of Christ, imitate God, and determine what pleases our Lord. This is a basic tenet of living the providential life.

We should also imitate and follow the example of those leaders that have taught us the Word of God (see Heb. 13:7). The good that has come from their faith is worth our consideration and recollection. The qualities these leaders exemplified are guideposts to Christian living.

> Dear friend, don't let this bad example influence you. Follow only what is good. Remember that those who do good prove that they are God's children, and those who do evil prove that they do not know God. (3 John 11)

Paul wrote to the church at Philippi urging them to follow their example. "Dear brothers and sisters, pattern your lives after mine, and learn from those who follow our example" (Phil. 3:17).

It is important for Christians to reveal the message of Christ in their lives. This can manifest itself in a variety of expressions and qualities.

> Let the message about Christ, in all its richness, fill your lives. Teach and counsel each other with all the wisdom he gives. Sing psalms and hymns and spiritual songs to God with thankful hearts. And whatever you do or say, do it as a representative of the Lord Jesus, giving thanks through him to God the Father. (Col. 3:16–17)

We are to live wisely and make the most of every opportunity to model Christ and reflect the qualities that he displayed.

> Live wisely among those who are not believers, and make the most of every opportunity. Let your conversation be gracious and attractive so that you will have the right response for everyone. (Col. 4:5–6)

The Holy Spirit that takes up residence in the believer allows the believer to live in the new way of living reflected in the life of Christ. The resulting Christian qualities give the believer new ways of serving God and living in the Spirit.

> And now you are united with the one who was raised from the dead. As a result, we can produce a harvest of good deeds for God. When we were controlled by our old nature, sinful desires were at work within us, and the law aroused these evil desires that produced a harvest of sinful deeds, resulting in death. But now we have been released from the law, for we died to it and are no longer captive to its power. Now we can serve God, not in the old way of obeying the letter of the law, but in the new way of living in the Spirit. (Rom. 7:4b–6)

Paul realized the power of using an example through tradition as a way to pursue a Christian life. "Now I commend you because you remember me in everything and maintain the traditions even as I delivered them to you" (1 Cor. 11:2 ESV). The Christian faith has been perpetuated through maintaining the teachings and traditions that originated with Christ. The qualities radiated to believers by the light of Christ have allowed this Christian tradition to be kept true to the faith. We should live our lives as Jesus did in obedience and imitation of the love and qualities Christ represented.

> And we can be sure that we know him if we obey his commandments. If someone claims, "I know God," but doesn't obey God's commandments, that person is a liar and is not living in the truth. But those who obey God's word truly show how completely they love him. That is how we know we are living in him. Those who say they live in God should live their lives as Jesus did. (1 John 2:3–6)

Paul urged followers of Christ to follow the example of himself and other leaders (see 1 Thess. 3:9). Christ explained that as he set the example that others are to follow. "I have given you an example to follow. Do as I have done to you" (John 13:15). Paul explains to Titus the importance of being an example to others.

> In the same way, encourage the young men to live wisely. And you yourself must be an example to them by doing good works of every kind. Let everything you do reflect the integrity and seriousness of your teaching. Teach the truth so that your teaching can't be criticized. Then those who oppose us will be ashamed and have nothing bad to say about us. (Titus 2:6–8)

The writer of the book of Hebrews reminds one of the importance of following an example of faith. "Remember your leaders who taught you the word of God. Think of all the good that has come from their lives, and follow the example of their faith" (Heb. 13:7). The qualities of providential living in Christ give us the means of perpetuating our faith to others, thus making possible the fulfillment of the great commission by creating disciples throughout the entire world.

CHAPTER FOURTEEN

Living Providentially

As we finish our study guide and journal on living a providential life, how do we go forward in a practical and comprehensive way to assist us in coordination with God's help to live our life in a synchronous path with God's will? All of the areas we have discussed in this book have pertained to God's will in our lives. The many Christian qualities have been used as an exercise for us to reflect the many dimensions of Christ's nature, character and outreach to believers.

What are the fundamentals as we go forth now in applying Christian qualities and everything we have learned about God's will in our lives? What structure can we use in our living a providential life? The following are life disciplines for the Christ–seeker to pursue the living of a providential life on a daily basis.

1. Bible study is one of the best ways to discover God's will in your life. One cannot hope to understand the ideas of God's will and providence without a fundamental knowledge of the Holy Bible. A daily regimen of reading a portion of scripture is recommended. All of the Bible is worth studying, although some is easier to absorb, understand and apply than others (see 2 Tim. 3:16). It is important to pray as a part of Bible study. Prayer allows the Holy Spirit to interpret and guide us in the process that He initiated. Other pertinent areas affecting your study will have God's help in your study through prayer, also. A concordance, Bible dictionary, and commentary can provide further assistance with the study and research process. A trusted Bible guide can be helpful as long as you don't restrict the scope of your study to certain books of the Bible.

2. Prayer is a necessary and powerful way to be guided in God's will. We are privileged to be able to communicate directly to our God through prayer. God holds our prayers in special regard and attention (see Rev. 5:8). God will shower you with grace and blessings in response to your prayers. We see throughout scripture that God listens to prayer and

even alters His course upon occasion in response to prayer (see Num. 14:20). Therefore, it is safe to assume that living the providential life is closely related and even dependent upon our prayers. One should use prayer in unison with your study of scripture to focus on the correct interpretation.

3. Attend church regularly. Church attendance fulfills a range of needs for every believer. The church is the body of Christ and is designed to be a home for all believers on earth. Worship is key to our relationship to God and church allows the fulfillment of this important process. Scripture, liturgy, sacraments, service, giving and preaching all are reinforcement of our Christian church worship functions.

4. Fellowship with other Christians regularly. An important assistance for any believer is to fellowship with other believers. This brings our Christian beliefs and living to a close and personal perspective. Accountability is maintained by regular Christian fellowship that serves the believer in their daily walk. We mature in our Christian walk through sharing our questions and experiences with other believers. This sharing can have a dramatic effect upon the providential path of our lives.

5. Don't just study and pray about God's word. Obey God's word (see James 1:22). The lessons of this in scripture are endless. "Praise the Lord! How joyful are those who fear the Lord and delight in obeying his commands" (Ps. 112:1). An important thing to strive for is to be obedient in the little things as well as the big ones. Our attention and reflection on our compliance with God's commands will pay big rewards and are part of our providential living.

6. We are to share our faith. Christ has charged us as Christians to witness to others. At the very earliest times of the church Christians were to witness to the ends of the earth (see Acts 1:6-8). It is therefore important for the Christian to be able to defend and share their faith at any opportunity. These opportunities can arise at the most unexpected times and last for only a fleeting amount of time that can be critical to the other person's eternal soul.

7. We are to develop and maintain a Christian attitude (see Eph. 4:23). Christian living requires a renewal of our thoughts and attitudes. We are to let the Spirit renew us. This will affect every aspect of our efforts to be more like Christ. Nothing can stop us from having a Christian attitude but ourselves. What a difference the attitude of a person seeking Christ can make in a life! A Christian attitude is naturally witnessing to the world at all times.

8. Place your reliance upon the Holy Spirit every day. Jesus sent the Holy Spirit to us when He went to heaven. Until Christ comes again, we can trust the Holy Spirit to convey Christ's communications to us (see John 16:15). Our reliance upon the Holy Spirit is critical in the face of challenges and the crises that we can often face. We can surely trust the Holy Spirit with our life's most critical decisions, disappointments, attacks and disasters. The Holy Spirit brings truth and power to the believer's life (see 1 Cor. 2:4–5,13).

9. We are to constantly seek and pursue Jesus Christ. The providential life for the believer is only realized when a person seeks Christ with all of their heart. When we live the Christian life to the full potential the heavenly rewards are impossible to imagine but as certain as anything we can believe (see Eph. 6:8).

10. We should have the firm realization that we are a child of God (see Gal. 4:7). This means that we are not just living in the time of an earthly life; but, we are already living an eternal life - now! This realization gives us a totally different perspective on the life of a Christian. This realization causes our faith, belief, obedience and actions to be framed in an eternal context.

Above are outlined ten fundamental areas of discipline for the believer to utilize in living the providential life. There are many more areas one could potentially explore in addition to these. The areas described above give a foundation of application that can be utilized for living a providential life for God. The application of these suggested items is exciting and full of energizing potential in the Christian's life. There is nothing revolutionary about any of these concepts. Scripture records all of these disciplines. It is when they are used in unity with the Christian qualities contained in scripture that they take on powerful potential for the believer. Implement these and see your spiritual life blossom. God's providence can reach a greater realization in our lives when we apply the qualities of a Christian's life. I hope you will make these qualities a part of living a providential life every day.

Printed in the United States
By Bookmasters